You Gotta *Get* UGLY

You Gotta *Get* UGLY

(U Gotta Love You)

Blodwen Hudon M.S.W.

ISBN 978-0-692-44736-9

Newdolb Press

Your children are not your children.

They are the sons and the daughters of life's

Longing for itself.

They come through you but not from you,

And though they are with you, yet they belong not to you.

You may give them your love, but not your thoughts,

For they have their own thoughts.

You may house their bodies but not their souls,

For their souls dwell in the house of tomorrow, which you

Cannot visit, not even in your dreams.

You may strive to be like them, but seek not to

Make them like you.

You are the bows from which your children as living

Arrows are sent forth.

Let your bending in the archer's hand be for gladness.

Kahlil Gibran, *The Prophet*

For Danielle,

Lost for too long,

And found forever.

$\int$

Contents

Chapter One

Madness and Magic

STICKS AND STONES will break my bones . . . She never broke my bones, only David's. He bolted when she was mad—out the door, down the garden path, scrambling up and almost over the back gate at King Edward Road, so close to freedom. One well-timed whack to his arm with the battling broom handle showed him who was in charge. Her five-foot frame barely battened down the bluster of an Irish woman fueled with anger, fierce as a fighting gladiator.

Running never occurred to me. Running was gutsy; I was not. Shrinking from her, maneuvering my arms awkwardly about, I sheltered what bits of my body I could. Furious hands landed everywhere, biting bare flesh like the wild, stinging nettles that caught me off-guard when I took short-cuts through the alley. Her children were the handy outlet for exasperation sparked by my dad, or by circumstances she hurdled daily for survival.

My body stayed put, and put up with it. My mind, however, had other plans; my mind could run. It switched off, and poof, like a magic act, it was gone, taking me with it. Where I went, what happened in my own absence is a mystery to this day.

The magic act began when I was five. We lived in Wales. My mother sent me to the shop with a half crown, a coin roughly the size of a silver dollar, no doubt to buy food. The coin was too pricey and too large to trust in my five-year-old hand, but she did.

Typically, I scavenged spat-out sweets from the ground, and that day was no different. Any reprimand she may have given

1

me to go straight to the shop and back vanished the moment I spied a sweet and stooped to pick it up. Focused, digging up the stuck sweet with my fingers, I dropped the half crown and watched in disbelief as it rolled to the edge of the curb, jumped off and plopped spitefully down the nearest drain—gone before I could make myself move. Crouching in the gutter, I stared into dirty water and the doom that lay ahead, my brain in a coma over the calamity that just occurred.

The voice in my head punished me before she did. *You're bad. You did it wrong. She won't like you.* I glanced around for a soft eye that might see the pickle I was in—but the queue squeezed under the bus shelter faced the opposite way. *No one is looking. No one will save me.* I cowered over the drain, afraid to move, delaying the inevitable.

There's no recollection of leaving that spot, no recall of the consequences once I arrived home minus the money and the food—blatantly bad, with no lie to hide behind. I'm tempted to say she killed me, but I'm still here and alive. From that moment on, my mind rescued me from anything threatening. And threats seemed to be everywhere.

Names will never hurt me... oh, but they did. When she shouted her loudest, any sane person would cringe. Thin lips scrunched in anger perilously close to mine, stiffened me like a corpse while death threats flew. They may not have been the obvious life-ending kind of threats, but to me they were. I was dead inside, in a way you could not see. The magic act had no power over words—but it wasn't simply the words—it was who said them and her tone of voice that made them arrows into my heart. I hurt myself with them more than she ever could, because I believed what she said in anger was true. Her words became the inner chatter I smacked myself with when she wasn't there. After all, whatever she dished out, I deserved. She knew me best. She was my mother.

One day, my anxiety was particularly paralyzing. I was in a narrow hallway trapped in a small, inescapable space—a tight corner between two doors, her face growling closer and closer to mine. All the muscles in my body tensed like a suit of armor on display in Warwick Castle. Instinctively my arm jerked up to protect myself and keep some space between us. My palm faced her; usually it faced towards me as I cowered. My back was up against the wall. This time, there was no room to cower. She was too close, too intense. I couldn't breathe. In that crowded moment, she must have thought I would hit her... If only I dared. "Don't raise your hand to me or I'll cut it off," she shouted.

I opened my mouth to attempt an explanation, although I knew better. She was fast. Not a single syllable escaped my lips. "Don't you dare talk back to your mother or I'll brain you," she threatened as she lifted a readied bent arm, her fist clenched tight. *She should give me a 'good hitting,' that's what I deserve.*

Sometimes the shouting and threats were it and nothing followed. But there was always a predictable next time. I waited for it to come but was never prepared when it hit. In retrospect, like David, I should have run. Chances are a broken arm would have hurt less than a broken spirit. However, in reality, David did not escape either. There were no lasting escapes.

I craved her approval, the way an addict craves their next fix. I wanted her to call me a *good girl:* then I could exhale, safe for the time being. Guessing what would please her never worked. *Nothing I do is ever good enough.* "You're no damn good," she'd say. *Yeah, yeah, I know. I've heard that so many times it's recorded in my head; I'm stupid, a fool, and I can't do anything right. What's wrong with me anyway? I'm big enough to know better.* Her unrealistic expectations of me became my unrealistic expectations of me.

Speaking up was not tolerated. Frequently, she told me to shut up. Her blitz of scathing words froze my mind's attempts to fend her off. *I can't think when she's screaming at me. I can't even move. I must have done something wrong.* Usually her tirades ended with, "Get out of my sight." I wanted nothing more than to be out of her sight *and* I desperately needed to be in her safe favor.

Emotional separation from my own mother, however, hurt like the worst sore throat I've ever had, and I had them often. Nothing made *me* feel better until *she* felt better, until she stopped being mad. More than once she came into the bedroom after her tirade. I wanted to believe she checked on me to see if I was alright. She did not come over to the bed, touch me, tuck me in, or anything of the sort. *I need to know that I'm safe. Please come over to me and make it better. She has to make the first move. She did not.* I pretended to be asleep. She left.

As I got older she would scan my face after every slap, perhaps to see just how far she could still push me until I showed her my backbone—perhaps wishing I had her mettle, perhaps disappointed I did not.

Ultimately, I pretended to be numb to her bullying and willed myself not to cry when she hit, denying her the satisfaction that she had power to churn me into emotional mush. But it was too late . . . the damage was done. *There's something about my own mother treating me like this. I must be worthless.* Raped of everything I needed to be me, my self-respect wiped off with every slap of her hand; if I ever felt worthy, the death threats chewed it up. I never knew a soul could be missing, but mine was. *I think God came and took it back. That's why I'm nothing.*

*

Perhaps her childhood was not so pretty either. At age fifteen my mother traveled alone from Ireland to England to look for work, apparently escaping an unbearable uncle upon whom she and her mother were dependent, and with whom they lived. Upon arriving in England, she lived in a convent with the nuns. She and my Welsh dad met in their early twenties as co-workers in a London hospital. They married within six months. I was the fourth eldest of eight children: four boys and four girls.

My dad was disinterested in family life. The discipline, decision making, and problem solving were hers, and hers alone, to shoulder. He was another child for her to deal with, an unruly one, as she could never control him as she controlled us. Although he lived with us, he was not a part of us. He was locked up inside and no one had the key, not even him. A father figure, he was never a dad.

She, on the other hand, could not be controlled by anyone. She was enviously wise, deferred to no one, never gave in and never gave up. By contrast, he was made of cardboard, and she was made of steel. Perhaps neither of them wanted children, but she was Catholic to the bone.

In the Irish and Welsh tradition, we called our mother Mammy or Mam. Patriotism, not blood, ran through Mam's veins. Vowing none of her children would first open their eyes in England, she journeyed by boat back to my grandmother's home in Ireland to give birth. Before my grandmother passed away, four children had been born in Ireland. The next three were born in Wales, and Gareth, the youngest, is a Coventry kid.

We moved from Wales to England when I was eight. Our first home, a three bedroom row house on King Edward Road in Coventry, was a good fit for a large family, until we took in lodgers—impromptu, not planned—Irish immigrants my mother found on the bus when she worked as a conductress. She simply bundled them up and brought them home. The rent money likely came in handy, but money was not her motive. She sorely missed her homeland and the familiarity of her country folk filled that void.

Mam always described herself as rough and ready. No standing on ceremony. No airs and graces. Take her or leave her. She had a big Irish heart, though. She would give the shirt off her back to anyone that needed it, even if it was her last.

Our house was amply and nicely furnished, with items purchased on the rent-to-own plan. Clean and organized, there were no frivolous items, no ornaments, except for a crucifix and a few religious pictures. It was never a jumble. Still, the front room was kept for company, primarily visiting Irish missionaries and Irish priests from the local parish. My mother always gave them a "good welcome," as she called it, with tea, sandwiches and biscuits.

Two double beds and a single one fit in the spacious, upstairs front bedroom. My parents' double bed sometimes ran alongside the wall with the door, and sometimes the headboard was against that wall with the bed facing the window. Joan frequently rearranged the furniture and my mother joked about not knowing where to find her bed when she came home from work. At times, my mother had a light-heartedness about her that brought spontaneous splashes of joy and temporary amnesia from fear.

Opposite my parents' bed, a delightful dressing table sat nicely in the arms of a bright bay window. Against an adjacent wall and to the left of the dressing table lay the double bed I shared with my brother David, the third eldest, and Clement who was younger than I. That bed never moved from its spot. To the right of the dressing table and opposite my bed was a miserable double-breasted, free-standing cherry wardrobe that gave me the shivers. At times there were more of us in our bed: some of us at the top and some of us at the bottom like sardines in a tin. A single bed ran lengthwise from the foot of our bed to the door. We often played musical beds, and as time went on it was hard to keep straight who slept where. At some point, Joan and Evelyn, the two eldest, shared the smaller second bedroom.

The bright bay window breathed life into that busy room. It breathed for me when scary things happened and I forgot how to breathe for myself. When the sides of the window were open, customary English net curtains flew freely like flags of surrender. I would have loved to surrender from that place, but there was nowhere else to go.

Bedtimes were scary. We weren't permitted to keep the light on. In the dark, the evil wardrobe's big eyes beamed. I knew it was watching me, which alone would have been frightening enough. *David says there's a monster under the bed with three eyes and two heads and it will rip me into bits if it gets me.* I cried. *He lays on top of me to hide me from the monster.* His private parts pushed against mine. Whenever someone downstairs switched on the landing light and started upstairs, he quickly rolled off.

One morning something was amiss. My pillow was damp; my hair felt stiff and crinkly as it did when I put goop on my fringe to make it straight. It was eerily quiet. I sat up, scanned the room, no one was there. A wet arc glared from the wall. I slept on the side of the bed away from the wall. *Did David stand on the bed, pee on the wall then turn his aim to me?* Too much to contend with, my body was instantly on its own. My mind whisked me away from madness, too depraved to make sense of any of it—I didn't have to remember any of it anyway—until years later.

Chapter Two

Dysfunctional Dynamics

IN THE DARKNESS of our bedroom, my parents engaged in a muffled sort of violence I later learned was sex. When I heard them scuffling in their bed I became anxious, afraid he was somehow hurting her.

Then there was their adult chatter, which made no sense at all. Mam said she knew about my father's fancy woman, Gwen. She said Gwen's children were the spitting image of us. She didn't raise her voice. She didn't have to. Her words dropped like acid. I imagined her lips pinched tightly together in precise anger, hardly space enough for words to slither through. *Why isn't she screaming at him? She screams at us when she's mad. Why us; why not him?* He was silent.

Of course, she never cried when she was wounded; gladiators are galvanized. It was obvious she was wounded. I felt it. I just didn't comprehend why. Squishing my face into the pillow, forcing myself to control the heaving in my chest, I cried as quietly as I could. *When she hurts, I hurt. I'm somehow tangled together with her and I don't like it. It's down to me to take care of her: but I don't know how. I cry because she doesn't, because I can't make her pain go away, because something's wrong and I don't know what to do.*

Mam eventually changed jobs from bus conductress to mail carrier and jokingly ate her breakfast of bread and jam before bed to save time the next morning. Her workday started at four o'clock in the morning, although busses didn't run that early. She walked a long way to work, whether or not the weather was inclement, whether or not she felt like it, even when she was sick.

In England we are used to walking—but her walk to work was over the top. *I'm afraid. How does she even dare to walk by herself in the dark? Why doesn't she say it's too cold, too wet, too creepy? I don't want her to be wet, or cold. Why does she have to be so tough? Why can't she take one solitary day off, just once, just because?* If she had, then I could at least have given myself permission to be human. *I don't measure up. Next to her I am a weakling, a failure.* Her daily mantra, "You earn your bread by the sweat of your brow," must have been her mainstay. She had the weight of eight kids around her neck. If she didn't work, we didn't eat.

When holes wore through the soles of her shoes, she padded their insides with cardboard until she could afford a new pair. After all, "Money doesn't grow on trees," and one of her children might need a coat, socks, or perhaps shoes. It seemed she scraped up enough money to buy a pair of shoes to keep one set of feet dry when another pair sprang a leak. She rated last. The truth is, she didn't rate at all. *My mother doesn't matter and neither do I.* She rarely, if ever, spent money on herself because her kids always needed something and physically, her kids came first.

My mother delivered mail on foot to city center businesses. I sometimes saw her when I took the double-decker bus into town. As the bus rounded the final corner into the city center, there she'd be, weighed down like a pack mule, slogging away, as if she were a man. It was both embarrassing and pitiful. Her short body teetered between two bulging bags stuffed with stacks of bundled mail, their straps diagonally across her chest—if one side was heavier than the other, she would have toppled over. My stomach hurt. *I feel sick! She shouldn't have to work like that. I am supposed to save her—but how? She's right; I am useless.* My mind switched off and the pain numbed.

The hefty mail bags left her round-shouldered. The consistent drenching of her uniform with rain no doubt contributed to her eventual arthritis. Often she was not there when I went to bed and hadn't returned home by the time I got up in the morning. She left the fire ready to light in the grate; all one of us had to do was strike a match and set the newspaper aflame. There was porridge with sugar and milk for breakfast, and she always managed to have school lunch money for us.

She picked up every overtime shift she could, working extra routes and sorting mail overnight. A mother hen, she foraged in the workplace for money, for sustenance for her chicks. She had eight mouths waiting at home to feed. She trusted, I suppose as a mother bird does, that her brood was safely protected in the nest while she was away—but I was not.

My mother hopped on and off buses for free, hurrying home between shifts to drop off food. Sometimes she stormed in agitated, primed to find something that rubbed her the wrong way, and sparks inevitably flew.

She might not notice me if I'm quiet. I was good at disappearing—melting into the wallpaper, in full view, yet invisible. It might have worked with others. I doubt it worked with her; nothing escaped her. Firmly planted for attack, head jutting from her body, furious words splattered everywhere, sticking to me like thick phlegm I couldn't wipe off. Genetically my brothers were safe—off the hook for chores because they were male. Yet, they were fair game for her anger and there was no shortage of that to go around. Her ranting over, she hopped on the next bus back to work. She could, of course, reappear at any time and unleash madness—or not. It was always a possibility.

The overhead light and cool air on my skin woke me. Squinting, I saw her, finally home from work, still dressed in that military-looking uniform, bending over me, engrossed in inspection. My scratching must have signaled her search. I watched her eyes tip-toe in step with fingers, deftly lifting up and putting down flannel folds of pajamas against my flesh. Her mouth slid from side to side the way it always did when she focused. She could have been a gorilla preening her young. Not the motherly preening sort, she was more like Special Forces in Vietnam stealthily maneuvering jungle foliage to root out the enemy.

The crisp click, click, click of squished red fleas between her thumbnails mimicked the rap-rap-rap of a rifle crackling in the night air. Once finished, her face relaxed. "Everything is under control," as she liked to say. Repositioning the various coats, which served as blankets, over me, she moved on to inspect my brothers. I fell back asleep content, knowing she would protect me from a flea or a warrior, knowing, without hesitation, she would sacrifice her life for mine. But when I really needed her to save me, she was never there.

Regardless of *why* we had fleas, it mattered *that* we had fleas. Can you imagine the shame I felt having coats for blankets, sleeping in a packed bed and fleas as well? If anyone had found out, I would have died right there. Fleas in our house, perhaps, came from multiple lost mutts led home by the soft-hearts of my siblings, Joan and David, suckers for stray pooches—and like our mother, stray people.

Our beds and bodies were scrupulously clean, teeth excluded. Toothbrushes and paste were not edible, so food came first. When our teeth hurt, socialized dentistry pulled them out. Like most homes of that time we did not have an installed shower. Mam took us to the baths on Coronation Road, the next street over, which was no doubt cheaper than firing up the geyser at home. The baths was simply a building with individual bathrooms. We were given a small bar of soap each and a white fluffy towel, water as hot as we liked and as much as we wanted, and a door with a lock. Going to the baths was a luxury I loved.

My mother dressed us from the second-hand shop, also on Coronation Road. A stuffy, angular, undersized front room was choked with dense layers of clothing dangling morosely from tired hangers, greedily puffed out from the wall, and sucking up all but a pocket of space in which to breathe. When my mother voiced her order, the round, wobbly woman shot upwards a long, hooked pole to rummage like a magic wand through hangers, surprisingly returning with the requested item. Buying clothes at the second-hand shop, to me, was a definitive disgrace. If my schoolmates found out, I would never have returned to school and the inevitable ridicule.

Twice Mam bought me new dresses for school events. One was unattractive but I pretended to like it. She had five pounds to spend—it cost five pounds. The other, a frilly pink dream, magically transformed me into a princess. My teachers' approving ooh's and ah's as they inspected the petticoats were far better than sweets. But the downside of glee was guilt. *You selfish brat! You don't deserve it. God knows how many hours of sleep she sacrificed to work overtime for that.* My mother was responsible for raising eight kids. My father was not. He acted privileged and single. He never set his well-shoed foot in the second-hand shop.

*

My mother was pregnant with Gerald, the third youngest, when my father, his floozy in tow, crashed his motorbike. She blamed his accident for the trauma that damaged their baby. My mother said Gerald's windpipe was not fully formed. Because of this he ate only certain foods. A curly blonde-haired, cherub-like, contented baby boy, there was a delicate aura of beauty and peace about him.

Aging slowly, he looked like a perpetual child. Joan looked after him—she loved him with a passion. Although I don't know precisely what, I now understand there was more to it than an improperly formed windpipe.

When it was time to place him in a children's home, my mother was devastated. She took us with her to visit Gerald; he lay on his cot, his wrists fastened to the rails to prevent him from scratching his sweet face. My mother did not like that one bit. It was upsetting for all of us and I would rather have stayed home.

I watched her intently during the visits. With a tenderness I never knew she possessed, she gently caressed the curly head of a son that never knew her, as if he were the most precious thing in the entire world. Crying, talking softly to him, she tenderly fed Gerald his favorite white chocolate. *She called him 'my darling.'* It was unmistakable. *She loves him. She can love. She just doesn't love me.*

David had a gentle, generous, playful side; he was easy to love. Artistic and creative, he even knew how to sew. As a mean streak emerged, however, it became increasingly difficult to find the good in him. When our parents were at work, David unleashed his violence on the rest of us. I remember laying on the kitchen floor crying, afraid to get up, certain I was cut in half after he rammed a garden shovel into my back.

Evelyn suffered from asthma, sometimes acutely, which made her seem frail. She never raised her hand or voice to anyone. Evelyn took meticulous care of her things and when Joan wore her clothes without permission my mother had a fit. When David punched Evelyn, Joan, the protector, stepped in. I have no doubt Joan saved me too when she was there. Joan was like our mother in that she refused to be intimidated.

David's stints in detention began early on; as an adult he was no stranger to incarceration. More than once policemen woke us at night looking for him, but he was elusive. My mother shipped him off to Ireland; he came back. When kids at school ran up to me after seeing his crimes in the newspaper, I lied and said he was not my brother: uncaring, they knew full well that he was. I wanted to escape from them and from the shame I felt, for if my brother did something bad, then so did I. I didn't know where David ended and I began.

Everyone saw my brother as a problem to be fixed, which shifted focus away from the dysfunctional dynamics of a family that, from outward appearances, seemed ordinary. Professionals looked at David's behaviors in isolation, but they were hatched in the context of family. The family was wanting; my brother was only the symptom, the scapegoat. This does not mean David is absolved from responsibility, however. Regardless of the influence of his upbringing, he is accountable for the actions he chose to take.

I stood in front of the dressing table mirror adjusting my grey school uniform skirt. It must have been cold, as the windows were sullen, shut tight that day. Someone came in; I turned towards the door, my back to the daunting wardrobe. It was David. Walking directly towards me, catching me completely off guard, he seized my shoulders and pulled me towards my parents' bed. If he spoke anything at all as I protested, I don't remember it. Resisting, I pulled back. There was nothing to grab onto on the wardrobe for leverage. I could not have held on anyway. I needed both hands in order to fight to free myself. I planted my feet on the floor; they did not stay put.

At that time, my parents' bed ran along the wall. There was no footboard in his way. The path to the bed was clear. The element of surprise was on his side. With whirlwind speed I was on my back on the bed, the right side of my body partially pinned down by his, my skirt quickly up above my waist. *Then* he was not *supposedly* protecting me from any monster. He *was* the monster. I was twelve.

He had never overpowered me before or even attempted to; I could not imagine his motive. But when my skirt was up and he wanted to yank my panties down, the realization that a boy, especially my own brother, would see my private parts made me fight with more fury than I knew I possessed. Beyond that, clueless about sex, I had no notion what he was up to. I was not quiet. I screamed and shouted for Evelyn.

Limp net curtains soaked up the insanity. Tightly-shut windows and well-built walls were on his side. No one could hear me—not even my brother. Nothing I said reached his brain. He was a mad man. I begged him to stop. I threatened to tell Mam. I threatened she would kill him, and she would have. I ordered him to stop. He didn't. He didn't care. *Where is Evelyn?* Any second I expected her to burst through the door and save me.

The fear I had of my mother, or anything for that matter, unmatched the inescapable, intolerable intensity foist upon me. Like a cornered animal, I fought off my own brother. My left hand was free, and with it I clenched the waistband of my panties with every ounce of energy I had to keep them up. His right fist grabbed tightly to yank them down. His hand was stronger than mine. He won. I lost.

Precisely at that moment, my mind once again snatched me away. I don't know what my brother did to me. I truly wasn't there. *No one saved me. Evelyn abandoned me, so did David, so did Mam, she was at work. She should have been at home, minding me.* The small voice in my head wanted to shoot me down for David's attack and sometimes I let it. *You should have been able to get away from him. You should have known how. It's your fault. You did it wrong. You should have tried harder. You let all of us down.*

The next thing I remember was walking downstairs, smoothing out my gray skirt, stuffing my white shirt into the waistband, straightening my blue necktie, detached from the violence as if it never occurred.

David stayed outside that evening riding his bike. I think he was afraid to come in and meet my mother's anticipated mood. I called to him, "David, I didn't tell."

Divorced from the trauma, I was loyal to the enemy. The putrid cohesiveness within our family once more left me taking responsibility for his reckless actions. I went through life with absolutely no conscious memory of that hideous day—until my thirties—then I remembered.

Chapter Three

Roots of Shame

MY FATHER WAS RAISED in Camarthen, South Wales, in a tiny village and a teacup of a house. He was one of nine children. In Camarthen, houses and cottages dotted the landscape, personalized with names instead of street numbers.

The coalmines suffocated my Welsh granddad with black lung disease when he was thirty-nine. I know nothing more about him.

Welsh Granny was stubby and wide like a dresser; her height was no match for her power. A strict, no nonsense matriarch, when she opened her mouth my dad jumped to attention. Granny could shout, and she did—at us.

Although her English was perfect, she chose to speak mostly in her native tongue. She did not speak directly to me, which was good: I was afraid of her. She talked about me to my parents in Welsh, as if I was not there—mundane chatter about how much I'd grown and so on, the gist of their conversations given away by my parents' gestures and comments.

Granny's skin was smooth and soft, her kind-looking face unwrinkled by time or worry. She would wear a black straight skirt hemmed below her knees, thick stockings and sensible shoes, her tidy white hair curled under at the bottom with pink rollers.

We did not visit Welsh Granny often enough to be close to her heart, and the same awkwardness I felt with my dad, I felt with her. I never hugged or kissed her either; she never hugged or kissed me. She had to make the first move: she didn't and I couldn't. My dad took after her. Maybe she never kissed or

15

hugged him either. Yet it was clear they loved each other; affinity was obvious on their faces, it sparkled in their eyes. *Their eyes never sparkle for me.*

The small house had a fireplace and no electricity. Somehow, her family all fit in there to sleep. Once that I recall, I slept there in a grand bed draped by ornate curtains. I pretended to be the Queen of England in Buckingham Palace. What, to me, was a big tin shed stood across from the small house. There the family cooked, ate and bathed in cold water under a tap that jutted from the wall. Prior to the tap, water was hauled from the village pump. The outhouse squatted near the end of a long path at the bottom of an adventurous garden near the crab apple trees.

Just because Granny told us to leave the apple trees alone didn't mean we would—not if we could get away with it, that is. Un-caged, cooped-up city kids, we ran free—as long as Welsh Granny wasn't looking. Getting into the car to leave, the stash of crab apples tumbled out from underneath my brother's jumper. It was hard to keep straight faces while Granny's upset face shouted at us. My usually stifled dad was mad. He shouted at us as we drove off.

After they married, my parents lived in Dundalk, Ireland. At some point they moved to Wales. My mother neither spoke nor understood Welsh. Wanting to be on a more equal footing with her in-laws and determined to learn their language, she would sit by the roadside with village kids after school in order to learn from them.

The in-laws did not like my no-nonsense mother, but eventually they respected her like a rattler. She was never their favorite person. They believed my mother made Dad's life hell. They had no idea that he never acted like a dad, a husband, or a father. He trampled our hearts, didn't even know we had hearts, and didn't seem to care.

On my mother's side, her father came from a wealthy family that forbade him to marry her mother, a mere farm girl. Undoubtedly, her disgraced mother endured moral crucifixion in 1917 Catholic Eire. My mother kept her illegitimate birth secret from us until we were adults. Then, out of the blue, after she'd had a drink, she mentioned it to Joan as if it were nothing.

She proudly reminisced that her father made sure she had the luxury of shoes in which to walk to school, while most of the village children went barefoot. She also told us that in spite of warnings to the contrary, her father printed retaliatory words against Ireland's enemies. He was shot to death execution style.

Perhaps in childhood, Mam was drilled in perfectionism to compensate for her shame-drenched birth. Regularly, she reminded us that we were a reflection of her, "Because you come from a big family, people will expect that you were dragged up and not brought up." Actually she said more than that but I stopped listening. My head was trying to deal with the grenade blithely thrown into my lap. *Did she just tell me not to show up the family: not to show* her *up?* Suddenly I was a mirror for the family. I reflected them. *If I look good enough, we look good enough, more importantly she looks good enough. I thought I already* looked *good enough. How do I* get *good enough? How do I know if I look good enough? What am I supposed to do?* Feeling good gave way to looking good.

It's no wonder kids at school made fun of me. They said I had weak genes because they were shared between eight of us. I believed them. Most of them were the only child in their polished families, and I was their shoddy contrast. Their mothers didn't work … mine never stopped working.

They already knew I was second-rate. They already knew my family didn't measure up. *They are right. I'm inferior.* I choked myself to keep every word inside, to not reflect more paucity on her, on us. *I'm ashamed of me, of my family. If only I was good enough, then my own mother might love me. I would do anything for her just to be nice to me, just to be glad to see me: not just because I got an A on my work at school, even if I dropped a plate and smashed it … even then. I want her. I want her to want me.* I hated that my parents had so many kids and that we were such an oddity.

Not only was I from a large family, my mother was Irish. Irish immigrant working men earned a reputation for congregating in pubs downing pints after a stiff day as navvy's (laborers), which most seemed to be. The Irish, in general, were viewed harshly. Hard workers without question; that ethic was well-entrenched in their collective character. Built as they were for toil and martyrdom, no wonder Mam never missed a day from work or complained about working. All the while, I senselessly suffered on her behalf—she likely was taking life in the stride that her proud heritage instilled in her bones.

*

With a knock-out smile and dashing good looks, my dad crooned like a pro, and he was masterful with the mouth organ. He serenaded at the packed Irish club in Coventry with poignant, lilting Irish lyrics that left no dry eye in the lot. And, of course, we learned Irish dancing there, which really was fun. In his younger days, my dad sang in the Eisteddfod, traditional singing festivals in Wales.

Dressed in a classy pin-striped suit and fancy leather shoes, my dad stole my breath away. No matter how much I craved my mother's love, I craved his more. At least I had her attention, albeit negative. He didn't know I existed. Maybe his heart was calcified—maybe it was just for Gwen. It seems absurd to say I lived in the same house as my dad and he spoke to me only twice in his lifetime. Patricia, my youngest sister, said he spoke to her once. I thought I was the only object of his disinterest. I was mistaken.

Tina, my neighborhood friend, lived down the street around the corner in the sweet shop her adoptive parents owned. Tina sat on her dad's lap, pouting. His arms cradled her, her head lay against his chest. His words soothing, he rubbed his hand up and down her thigh, smiling and patting her like a puppy. Holding my breath, I watched transfixed in near disgust as that kind of closeness seemed a sin. *How can a man, her own dad, be that affectionate? It's not right. He's not her real dad though. He's a fake dad. Tina must have been an orphan. Her real parents probably died in a car crash, her relatives must all be dead too. That's how you get to be an orphan. That's how you get to be adopted.*

My dad was not a real dad either; he was a stranger that I called Dad, safe to covet only from a distance. There was no alcohol in our house, ever—all his drinking was done at the club. Some Sunday afternoons he would sit in his chair by the fireplace, beer plainly on his breath, while we all watched television together. I swear we were the last family in England to get a television, and when we finally did, it was thrilling.

Sitting on the couch, from the corner of my eye I monitored my dad's every move. When he laughed at *Old Mother Riley* films, I laughed because he did, and in those few seconds as he glanced around the room to see who was sharing his glee and catching my eye, there was no separation between us. I glowed; he didn't even notice.

I watched him, because at any moment the unexpected could occur. I watched in order to be quick to make the right move at the right time: to be ready to please, to be good enough for my dad to love. *I'm never good enough for him either.* When Tina's dad caressed her I didn't recognize it as love. How could I? I thought I was special because my dad named me after his sister who died in infancy. I was wrong. I was simply child number four—if he ever counted.

A city bus driver, my father was also the elected, unpaid secretary of the bus company's Workingman's Club. Gwen lived across the street from the club and worked for the bus company collecting fares. When Dad arrived home from the club drunk, his face was wild. He screamed vicious words at my mother almost without stopping, spit whipping itself into white froth in the corners of his deranged mouth like a dog we once had with distemper.

He was the cheater, but he projected his infidelity onto my mother. Ridiculously, he accused her of running around with an odd little fellow that would never have turned my mother's head. Besides, she had no time for shenanigans, she had us. Anger consumed him and he exploded, arms and fists swinging like a madman's until policemen pried him off her. Joan sometimes jumped on my father's back to save my mother. I fell back into shock, into mindlessness.

None in our house ever talked about the violence. Each time it occurred, it was terrorizing, and each time felt like the first time. When it was over, it was as if it never happened.

I watched as my mother prepared and served my dad his favorite yellow fish, which she purchased on a break from work, rushed home, cooked and then rushed back. *He hit her. She is the victim here. Why is she waiting on him hand and foot? Why is she the one always making it better?* There was no obvious glimmer of affection between them, just faces with war paint wiped clean and a sense of satisfaction and contentment that quietly pleased them both as if serving and being served, atonement and absolution, mended it all.

Policemen had rushed right past me the night before, each with a hand on his helmet holding it in place, their long legs taking our stairs two at a time, stairs my dad tried to push my mother down. They hurried to save her from a lunatic.

Surely, it was not my dad who was wreaking havoc. Surely, he was not the one that smashed the toys set out for the younger ones for Christmas morning, and beat up my mother. It *looked* like my dad at the top of the stairs in a volcanic rage, in his bus driver's uniform. I saw the reflection of silver buttons bounce off black clothing shiny from wear. His hair was dark. He had a moustache, glasses too. But my dad was a quiet man. The man at the top of the stairs could not be him. The man I worshipped in my heart, whose love I longed for, slammed Mam with awful words. He lunged at her like a wild animal about to tear apart his prey.

My dad was two people—nasty and nice. My mind predictably flipped me to his nice side: the mute, sometimes smiling side. My father beat up my mother, and she went out of her way to reward him. It was easier to pretend nothing bad happened than to make sense of that scenario. Perhaps my mother couldn't reconcile his two sides either. Perhaps like me, she forgot the nasty when he was nice. Perhaps he apologized while I was off with my galloping mind.

My mother had grit. Her survival, and ours, depended on it. Only once did I see her cry. Of course we cried too, huddling around her on the floor, our jumbled arms competing for space to hang around her neck, dangling from her like the yoke we were. "Men are no good," she said, "They only want one thing." Not knowing precisely what she meant, the grudge in her voice made them words to remember. They stuck with me like a mantra.

Bogged down with eight kids, she was tied to an unfaithful, abusive man. I never heard her say she wanted to leave him or that he should go. *Why not?* She never once wished out loud that we weren't born, said we were a burden or blamed us for the hours she worked to keep us warm, dry and fed. I wanted her to be angry and lash out until she felt better. As long as she was tough there was hope; we would at least be alive. *I need her to protect me.* Equally my protector and my slayer, I knew that she would never maim me or kill me in a way that I would physically die. Strangely enough, she was my existence—she was my ticket to life.

Mam had an array of off-putting facial gestures; they were part of her arsenal of defense. I see them now as quills on a porcupine—stay back or be skewered. She wore one of them the day she swished through the front door from work, went directly into the front room, opened the door into a small cupboard under the stairs where the gas meter was mounted on the wall and emptied the coins from the meter. We paid for electricity as we used it, plopping shillings into the meter as needed.

Desperate and scraping for money, for there was never enough, she put herself on the firing line with my dad, trying to get what she needed. Seething, thin lips scowling, her chest heaved, scantily repressing its rage: white strapping tape covered her thumb. Mute, she ignored me as I stood watching.

Assuming her fury had to do with her thumb, I didn't fear that she would hurt me, yet I was afraid. Concern for her injury gave me the gumption to ask, "What happened to your thumb?"

"Swine." She pressed the word with familiar emphasis through gripped teeth. "Your father broke it." *Why did she say 'your' father? Why didn't she say 'my' husband? Is it my fault?* My mind went into magic mode. I don't remember the rest of the conversation, if there was one. I suppose she either asked him for money and he refused, or she threw Gwen in his face as a last resort. Another swish and she was gone.

I imagined my mother's intimidating Irish mouth to be a double-edged sword of destruction and defense, an icon that scared away danger the way a crucifix banished vampires. Fearlessly, she wielded her weapon, uncaring of whomever it sliced and diced. Not even the revered priest was safe if he crossed her, which he sometimes did.

In reality, in spite of her weaponry of words, she was simply a woman pitted against a man—no more than a fragile, dry twig easily snapped beneath his masculine combat boot. *If she's not safe, neither am I. Will he kill her? Who will save us? Will he break my bones? Will he kill me? Will it be today?*

*

We lived in Wales when she wore red lipstick and went out for the evening with my dad. Her puckered lips kissed the air near me as she left. *I was right there with my mouth ready and she didn't even kiss me.*

Without question, my mother made tremendous sacrifices for all of us. Day after day she put her "nose to the grindstone," as she called it. *Surely she would not have struggled so unless she loved me. But there is not one single thing I can point to that proves her love. Things are not love. She has obligations. I am one of them. I am a burden.* As I look back now, her unending quest for our physical survival left no time for the niceties of love that mattered—tender actions and words that make love unmistakably that. Busily focused on feeding eight mouths, my mother inadvertently starved eight hearts.

Hustling home between shifts, she hastily unpacked the post office bag bulging with marked-down, bruised fruit from the market. When her mood was sober, I wished she would stay. I wanted her—not crummy apples in her place: not food to fill my belly so I wouldn't feel the pain. *I want her. I can't have her. Stop wanting ... Just stop!* But my heart was too smart to speak up. I said nothing. I let her go. She ran back to her priority, back to work. *She left me ... again.* She worked double-time to feed my body and all my heart wanted was her.

I hated that thing called money. No matter how much she struggled and sacrificed to get it, it never stretched far enough. When my father refused to give her money she forged his personal checks, yet the bank always spotted it. She said everything was under control, but it wasn't. I heard apprehension behind her words. And I watched wizardry wave her Irish eyes about, scheming up a solution. Would her solution appease him? Would he remember the appeasement when he was besotted with booze? Would he bash her anyway? Money in my house was mixed-up with violence. My dad never grasped the cost of raising his kids.

We lived on King Edward Road for five years before selling the house and buying another, yet memories of that place fit into the palm of my hand—they are unsavory ones, except for ice cream. Sometimes on Sundays when she was home, Mam would send us to the ice cream shop, or out to the ice cream van in the street with a plump, thick-lipped, ornate, pale green, tiny-flowered pot reminiscent of the chamber pot kept under the bed in Wales. When the pot was filled, the server dribbled our favorite raspberry ripple over the white mounds of creaminess. Sugar was more than sweet to my tongue. Sugar coated inside pain.

Other moth-eaten memories are from subsequent houses: my brothers scarfing down a whole loaf of white bread in one sitting; and whoever got to the bottles first of unpasteurized milk on the doorstep, siphoned off their creamy tops. Our food was plain, our staple: spuds. I remember sugar sandwiches; burned fingers from toasting bread on a short dinner fork at the fireplace; and Joan deviously teaching me how to toast bread with the iron when my mother was not around.

My mother could fix anything physical. If it was emotional, it didn't exist. She made us a bed on the couch when we were sick and spoiled us with special food and drinks. If it required making six quick trips a day home to check on us, she did. She carried me up and down stairs when I had rheumatism and couldn't walk. Maybe I got rheumatism on purpose. She was forced to touch me then. But it was a somber carrying—not a loving one. *She's just going through the motions: handling me like a sack of mail she's vacantly bundling up, getting this job done so that she can run back to the other.*

She never complained or scolded me for getting sick, being a nuisance or creating more work for her. *She never kisses anything better. She never hugs or soothes anything away.* She brought me things then left, disappearing into the drone of survival. *Loving must be a luxury left to mothers with time to spend it, to mothers who do not have to work, to mothers that have one child, maybe two. But she can love. She loved Gerald. Why not me?*

When I tripped over the clothesline prop on the back garden path, splitting my chin open on a paving stone, she marched the two of us a couple of miles to the hospital. Everything in her life was fast-paced—no lollygagging allowed. She clutched one of my hands, and with the other I squeezed a rag tight against my chin, running to keep up with her. The rag turned red. People gawked as we passed, unasked questions on their faces.

Gareth climbed onto an outbuilding as we crammed against the railway fence to catch a glimpse of the queen in the passing train. The chimney stack collapsed on his hand and without missing a beat she grabbed him, his severed half thumb, and ran for help. Although she was fast, his thumb could not be reattached.

David held a firework too long and it exploded in his hand; she was called to the hospital. Joan was speared in the thigh by a spike as she climbed over the back fence; my mother left work and came home. My mother's life with eight kids was a series of emergencies that summoned her from work. Without getting angry, she did whatever it took to deal with the crisis, then promptly returned to work.

A goose, probably for Christmas dinner, fully feathered, neck and head dangling but intact, hung on a hook inside the pantry door. As we cautiously looked at it, squirming, Mam slipped it off the hook and chased us around the house. We scattered, squealing with delight and disgust when she almost caught us. Then we all pitched in at the kitchen sink and de-feathered the goose. Playful times were sparse, magical: I felt relieved and happy.

With the birth of Gareth, the youngest, came my mother's diagnoses of cervical cancer. I watched a once robust woman practically drag herself up the road from work. The radium treatment knocked the life out of her even though its purpose was to save it. Somehow, she put one foot in front of the other and kept going. Clement said dad took him to the hospital to say goodbye to her as she was not expected to live.

Thanks to my mind's magic act I have minimal memory of that time. The doctor ordered Mam to a convalescent home at the seaside and after a bit of much-needed physical rest, she told the disease, in her words, to "bugger off." With neither time in her life, nor space in her mind to entertain a prolonged illness, she came home cured. If anyone could make a shift with sheer resolve, it was my mother. She was a survivor.

Chapter Four

No Safe Place

CARDINAL WISEMAN CATHOLIC SCHOOL was tuition free, initially girls only, and most of the teachers were nuns. School was a nightmare. Quiet, unassuming and filled with fear, I constantly hid inside myself hoping I wasn't so translucent that these kids, with one look, would see how different I was from them—how freakish my life really was. *I'm such a mess, and so is my family. I don't fit in. I don't belong anywhere.* Despite my best efforts to hide, I attracted what I loathed: attention, and negative attention at that.

In the compulsory sewing class, I was required to make my summer uniform dress. The lay teacher, mean-spirited and sharp-tongued, was the only person whose lungs outdid my mother's. Faster than Billy the Kid with a six gun, she pulled out a ruler from nowhere to rap disobedient knuckles. According to her, my knuckles were incorrigible. Sometimes she stood at the classroom door crowing, her mouth gyrating like a gymnast on fast forward, eye glasses on the precarious end of her bent nose teetering as she ranted, welcoming me with a whack of the ruler that stung my pride more than it stung my hand.

She did not like me, and the feeling was mutual. Inability in her class translated to insubordination. She took it personally. I was her example to the class of how not to sew. "You're doing it wrong. Rip it out...rip it out...rip it out..." she'd screech, her face coloring like a rooster's comb. Then she'd point to and praise my classmates—those with talent. Not only were their dresses finished fast with accuracy and ease, they made nice, non-school clothing of their choice during class. *They are better than me. They can. I can't.*

The dress was complicated. Small checkered material meant matching up squares at those never-ending seams that got me into endless trouble. Buttons, button holes, sleeves, gathered waist, a collar, none of which I had experience sewing, demanded precision. Being a novice was without merit; there was no margin for error. *I should know how, and I don't. What's wrong with me?*

As she stood over me shrieking, my mistakes multiplied. Not only did I pick out the tiny stitches as ordered, I missed the thread and picked holes in the material instead. Covering up what I could with my hands as she made her rounds, I prayed she would not stop at my desk and closely stick her nose into my work. Finally, she approved the stitching and I wore the dress.

Unbelievably, sewing is one of my passions today. She taught me to do good work, to be precise. Once I was aware of it, I saw that mismatched squares really did look unsightly.

Sewing wasn't my only challenge. I couldn't get my mind around math, so Sister Agnes parked me outside the classroom door; I suppose to learn by Divine intervention. According to Sister Agnes, I needed to *apply myself.*

Thoroughly frustrated with my deemed laziness, she marched me to Mother Coleman, the Headmistress, for rebuke. *Is she stupid? Punishing me is not helping. I'm not messing up math on purpose. I just don't get it.* At least with sewing, I understood the problem and learned to correct it. Sewing made sense—math did not. *I can't do it. There is something wrong with me.* Tutoring made no difference either.

The nuns loved quiet; disobedience was not tolerated. Sister Agnes could zap me with a look so effectively damning that there was no need to raise her voice or hit, and she did neither. When the look landed on me, my eyes dropped from hers, shot downward to my desk and tried to crawl inside, taking me with them. I wanted approval from Sister Agnes more than I wanted air. I was a good girl. *She must know I'm a good girl—I'm quiet.*

Perched on a pew with her cohorts, she saw me at morning mass during the week and at confession on Saturdays with

Gareth, the toddler, in tow trying to control him as he ran up and down the aisle, showing me up every time. At home and at school, the common denominator and the price tag of survival was quiet. *Quiet equals good. Be seen and not heard. Better yet, be invisible.*

Sister Agnes taught us that pinching cheeks and biting lips to give them color was all the make-up we needed. "Young ladies never wear skirts above the knee or cross their legs except at the ankles." Although she never uttered the word "sex," clearly there was something bad and wrong with boys and having babies. "Getting pregnant is always the girl's fault," she cautioned. Dead serious when she spoke, the bit about blame stuck. The rest was beyond me.

When my mother would introduce me she added, "She's shy," as if pointing out a crippled leg or some physical defect to be pitied, never mentioned—lowering their expectation of me, in case they had any. *I'm so furious with you. Why did you say that? Stop telling people there's something wrong with me. I'm trying to look normal. I am not shy.*

Inside-screaming was the best I could do. Talking back or speaking up was out of the question. *I'm quiet, there's a difference.* I trained myself to be quiet out of fear of reprisal and fear of being seen inside this skin of mine. Being quiet is as hellish as speaking up; they are equally evil, equally anxiety ridden. *I can't wait to escape and be by myself.*

Mostly my conversations were between me and the small voice in my head—essentially me talking to myself. That was not always safe either. The small voice had a mean tongue. Presumed shyness was a great hiding place for a running-scared kid like me … until it turned into my prison.

My mother said precisely what was on her mind, unedited, to others, just as she did with us. I shook in my shoes; spit collecting in my throat that I was too mortified to swallow. She might see my Adam's apple move, turn her attention from the others to me, then pounce. Because my stomach twisted, I assumed theirs did too.

Then there was Dad. Mam's words knifed him. Well-oiled with alcohol, he would punish her with a startling stash of saved-up anger. He hit me once that I remember: a blazing backhand across the face from nowhere. Once could be twice or even more. *I'm not safe ... from anyone. Life is not safe.*

I never wanted to be like my mother. I never would be. I had different stuffing. She had nerve, I had nice. I was nice when I didn't want to be. I had programmed myself to please.

Chapter Five

Sweets and Sorrow

I WANTED TO BE one of the kids with lit-up faces that packed the sweet shop after school. When I spied five shiny shillings on Lily's desk, I impulsively lifted it. *I have to be sneaky to get what I want. I'm bad inside and just pretend to be good. Good is protection, like armor.*

My mother did not buy sweets except at Easter: traditional boxed chocolate eggs, one for each of us, decorated with colorful pretty flowers made of icing. When the lodgers sent me to the shop across the road to buy their cigarettes, I brazenly bought sweets too. They looked at their change, then at me and never questioned it. Having experienced no real consequences for my actions distanced me from the reality that I was stealing.

Hungry for the escape sugar gave me; the actions I took were reckless. Two weeks after I stole her lunch money, Lily, perfectly healthy one moment was suddenly dead the next. That registered. That was a turning point. That consequence was hefty—I was marked for hell.

The school must have notified my mother when Lily's money went missing. Kids from school probably saw me having a spending spree in the sweet shop. It was playtime when I glimpsed her marching into the principal's office. Of course, she bulldozed them with threats: "I'll have your guts for garters." My mother's mere angry presence twisted my intestines; I never knew what to expect from her. Sure that she verbally flattened them like pancakes in that office, and stood like a steel girder supporting me, made no difference.

None dared slight her offspring and get away with it! Whether or not I was guilty was immaterial. If I was accused, so was she. Her honor and integrity were dulled and she would have none of that. She was there to preserve *her* face not mine. If my mother asked me about Lily's money, I lied. *Good is safe. Bad is not.* All in all, I did not feel backed by her display of bravado that day; her raucous behavior didn't help me or my image one iota. I was still afraid, still guilty, and I still needed five shillings.

Traditionally at Christmas time, children went house-to-house singing carols. Somehow carols always sound good even when, like me, you can't sing, and there were always two or three of us, which helped. The spirit of the season mattered, not the quality of our voices. After delivering a couple of carols, a quick knock on the door brought the reward of a handful of coins. Seldom did a voice from inside shout out, "Not tonight!" Toes frozen, fingers cold, nose red and runny, my pockets filled with jingling loot, I stopped on the way home to buy bags of salt and vinegar crisps, to keep me company while I excitedly counted out coins on the kitchen table. The money made it all worthwhile.

Father Christmas brought girls in our family each a doll and a long black stretchy nylon stocking bumpy with nuts and fruit. Our search party led by Joan unearthed the hidden dolls well before Christmas stuffed behind the dangling, alien-faced gas masks in the back of the cupboard on the upstairs landing. Thank heaven for Christmas, and carols, and finally five shillings, which I gave to the priest to say a mass for Lily's soul. I was, at last, out from under God's vengeful thumb.

My mother's next school visit was quite different. The class assignment was to write letters to the newspaper opposing the showing of X-rated films in town; mine was published. When my teacher, with the priest, acknowledged me in class, their praise was eclipsed by a careless comment and chuckling, "You should have an Irish name like Mary O'Brien so that people know you are a Catholic girl."

Mam was a fighter on the lookout for a cause; disparage me you disparage her—watch out! Her schooling was minimal; her grand wit and wisdom could never be gleaned from books. She occasionally misspelled my name, yet none would besmirch it or chuckle for long.

Barging up to the front of the classroom, she planted herself threateningly only inches in front of my teacher's face and flapped her finger. From a puckered mouth that meant business, in front of everyone, she gave my teacher a "piece of her mind," as she called it. She was there about my identity, not my behavior. She was there about me and she protected me. I felt it. I loved it. A big smile curled up on my heart and kicked back, whistling.

Doing well in school had its reward: my mother's approval. Our education was important to her. She excused me from doing dishes to do homework, making Joan do them instead. Joan was not a true fan of school. She had other plans and conforming wasn't one of them.

Joan preferred to be earning money and took on more than one job, even as a kid. A hard worker like our mother, Joan had no lazy or visibly scared bone in her body. No matter the job, she could turn her hand to anything. If it paid wages, she did it, and well. When Joan worked at the cake shop she bustled home like our mother, with bulging bags of unsold bread and yummy fresh cream cakes crammed in her arms. In the chaos of childhood, a fresh cream cake was a delectable detour.

Even though we grew up together in the same house, I have no memory of Patricia. Whatever I know about the two of us growing up, she told me later. I've since learned that I bossed Patricia: made her put her school beret back on in public; told her to stand up straight; properly enunciate her words; and more. I suppose pecking order power was the only control I had. Or was I making sure she looked good enough… that she didn't show me up? I think I took on an air of haughtiness, hoping it made me look good.

In spite of all that, she was nice to me. At night, when my asthma flared up and I struggled to breathe, she propped me up in bed with pillows. Loving is second nature to Patricia. It's a mystery where she found that non-belly-filling staple so elusive to us as children. Even today, she has an unlimited supply and gives it away to everyone, everywhere. My sisters are the gems in my life.

Following my school completion ceremony my mother took me to the club to see my dad. He accessed rather fancy, pint-sized beer mugs gifted by the breweries, some of which came home. I prize the ones I still have.

That night I couldn't tell if he was drunk or sober. He stood, face flushed crimson, sucking on a cigarette buried in the yellow nicotine-stained fingers of one hand, white knuckling his pint with the other. Suddenly, his pint-sized glass sped through the air along with others; beer rained down, tables overturned, and he wrestled in a boozy brawl that seemed to brew from nowhere. That must be the frightful ring where he honed the punches he brought home to my mother. We left, stopping at the fish and chip shop for chips and mushy peas before hopping on the bus home.

*

Joan woke me in the middle of the night to help her clean the house as a surprise for our mother when she got up for work the next morning. I wonder if it ever paid off, or saved my hide.

Chronologically fifteen going on ten, Joan used to take me dancing with her. She rode home with a fellow she liked, and his friend offered to drive me. He pulled over before we got to my house, lunged at me mauling my neck before I could push him off. Locked out by our mother because we were late, Joan and I squeezed, in blackness, through the tiny pantry window in the conservatory, giggling like fools as knocked-over tins clattered to the floor, fear of next day repercussions forgotten for the moment.

The love bite glared back from the mirror. *She'll kill me. I'll cover it up with make-up before she gets home tomorrow.* I learned the hard way that my mother made a head count before dawn, before leaving for work. Seeing my neck, however, she stripped off the covers shouting, and stingingly slapped me awake. She would have no tart's trademark on her daughter. *I'm too old to be hit . . . I want to tell her to stop.* Somewhere I had lost the right to stand up for myself. It eroded ever so slowly, and surreptitiously I hardly noticed it happening. I lost the ability to be heard. I learned to have nothing to say. I learned to just take whatever happens. I learned to be quiet. I let quiet happen.

When my mother next raised her hand to strike me, I raised mine against her for the first time. I didn't put my hand down and she did not tell me to. She was just as staggered as I that I would ever dare threaten her. Someone else stood rock solid inside my skin. That person was not backing down. Shock froze us both. She looked straight at me and I looked back. Her enquiring eyes ambled around assessing the situation, weighing up her next move. She no doubt saw the odd trance in eyes not mine that day. Whatever possessed me had gall enough to take on my mother, however it played out. Her hand went down—she never raised it to me again. The words, if any, and what came next, are lost to me. It was a small victory, if a victory at all. She was still powerful and in control. I was still unvoiced, and still afraid of her.

At sixteen I worked full-time, paid room and board to Mam and bought my own clothes. In a chic boutique in town, I fell in love with a pricey designer suit, the perfect shade of green that exactly matched my eyes. A size too small, the saleswoman convinced me it fit. Although I knew otherwise, feeling pressured, I bought it. *I can't say no. I don't stand up for myself and hate myself for it.* My mother was upset at the saleswoman for selling it and with me for buying it. "Speak up for yourself," she said. She didn't get it. Time made the childhood knot in my vocal cords too tight to untie. I was petrified to return the suit; I was petrified not to. Reluctantly I went back to the shop. The woman refused to refund my money, so my mother stepped in. Of course, she came home with the cash.

Many backed away from my mother's spirited words; few dared take her on toe-to-toe. Others loved her and laughed at her humor. She had a way with words that could entertain and charm. Others could not get enough of her saucy mouth and colorful, novel stories. She epitomized the wisdom, determination and valor of which they only dreamt. They valued her strength, spark, and spirited, feisty fearlessness. The more she scorned their opinions and comments, the more they adored and admired a candid, unabashed honesty they would never have. They knew just where they stood with her. They loved it. They loved her.

*

Evelyn lived in another part of the country and, as was customary, boarded at the hospital where she worked as a nurse. She never let asthma stand in the way of her passion for nursing. During a visit home Evelyn had an asthmatic attack: nothing new for her. Her pills and inhaler had always worked in the past and she always recuperated. I wasn't worried, clueless this time was different, serious.

Dispatched to walk up the road to the doctor's office, doing precisely what a sixteen going on ten-year-old would do, I jumped on and off the sidewalk; balanced on the edge of the curb; skipped; and took my time. If I brought medicine back it did not work. Someone, perhaps Joan, was on the phone asking Mam's boss to find her and send her home—it was an emergency. My mother arrived. The doctor came. Evelyn sat on the couch. He bent down and gave her an injection. The air was jello—suffocating. No one spoke.

The hushed voices of my parents woke me as they checked on Evelyn before going to bed. She had been laboring for air while I slept soundly in the bed next to her with Patricia. *I should have known. I should have heard her.* Panic squelched all breath in the room, or was it only mine? Patricia and I watched as ambulance men carried her downstairs. At the bottom of the stairs her arms flung themselves about. They tied her to the stretcher. It was frightening to witness. Her body was there, Evelyn was not. She slipped into a state where she couldn't be reached. I suggested we pray the rosary so that Evelyn would be home for Christmas.

There was no oxygen in the ambulance, and my sister died in my mother's arms as the ambulance rounded the first corner. It was the twenty-second of December. My sister was twenty-three years old. I went to work the next day as if nothing happened. When I told co-workers my sister passed away, their eyes widened. "Why was I at work?" they asked. My heart and head were disconnected. The world had ended.

My mother said Evelyn was our father's favorite. I could tell my father had been drinking. He sat on the couch beside my mother clinging to her, crying like a baby, fondling her breasts—a little boy looking to his mother for comfort. It seemed perverted, but she did not stop him. My parents had each other in a sick kind of way. We neither had them nor each other. *Why him and not us?* We did not console or comfort one another even in that tragedy, because we didn't know how. Our role models were emotional cripples with kids' feet in adult shoes. I learned by example to be emotionally unavailable—even to myself. *Be tough. Being vulnerable is being weak; it's just not safe.*

Somehow each of us kids managed to muddle through childhood alone using whatever coping skills we could find, and that worked. We did not collaborate, band together, talk about anything, or trust. We endured, we saw, we kept everything to ourselves. We were strangers, solitary soldiers, each of us standing at our own guard-post waiting for the next missile in the war zone called home.

When Joan came home at night and heard our parents fighting, she sat outside on the wall, or left. Patricia, who convinced herself there was a mix-up at the hospital and she mistakenly ended up in our family, would hide for hours in the pantry holding Joan's half-blind Pekingese dog, Bobsy; crouch under the ample kitchen table; or sit on the wall down the road. I have no idea how my brothers coped except for David; he rebelled. Without the wherewithal to hide somewhere else, I hid inside myself; after all, I had a magic mind. And therein lay the problem—there was no door to me to open, peep around, or sneak out of when the coast was clear. Sneaking out of me was tricky. *How do I know it's safe?*

When bill collectors banged on the door, I cringed and hoped I would not be the one made to answer. Whoever answered the door recited the instructed spiel: said that my mother was not there, even if she was; promise the bill had been paid; or would be paid the next payday. My mother paid her bills, just not always on time, and she never made trivial purchases.

When a couple came to the door asking for my mother, not money, and returned a second time, curious, my mother answered the door herself. They were from the children's home. Gerald had died from pneumonia. Buckled by shock, almost collapsing, my mother wailed with inconsolable grief. Brokenhearted, still mourning Evelyn's death just two months previous, how was she supposed to deal with the devastation of a daughter taken before her time, and then so soon, a son? Gerald was declared an angel and his life was celebrated with a votive mass of the angels. The priest told us to dress in white, not black. Still, it was a funeral, the death of a child—the death of *her* child.

*

Twice a week I went dancing at the Locarno with a friend from work—an in-crowd girl. We were total opposites: she, an only child with everything she wanted; me, the poor kid from a large family faking *good enough*. I met Keith at the Locarno. We were eighteen. He was my first boyfriend, my first love, my first goodnight kiss. Two years later we planned our engagement, but life had other plans.

Late one night, sitting on his knee in my mother's kitchen, my world crumbled. Egged on by friends that were sexually active—he wanted us to go all the way. Naïve and unclear precisely what sex was, I knew it was off limits, even sinful until marriage, when it surreptitiously became acceptable. Keith's words were soft and caring yet I felt my heart break in two. He was asking me to do what I could not. It was over. We both cried. Tears glued our cheeks together for the first and last time.

I lived at home, the norm for young adults. Accountable to my mother and living under her roof, her values owned me. Heaven forbid I was on my own somewhere in an apartment: I might not have been so strong. I might have surrendered to him. I loved him and missed him terribly.

My mother was my strength. She did the thinking for both of us. Like a well-trained puppet, whatever she told me to do I did, whether I wanted to or not. Whether she was right or not, she was always right. *I didn't want him to leave me, but he did. He left because I was good. If I had been bad, he would have stayed. I want to be bad, but I can't be.* The only private place to mourn was on the upstairs landing. I lay there often, crying . . . and I cried at work. No matter how much I cried, the hurt stayed the same.

The pain of losing my first love was nearly intolerable. Wherever I went socially, there he was, and usually with a date. I couldn't take it. Skimming through a magazine, an advertisement for job opportunities overseas as an *au pair* jumped off the page. What a perfect solution. My work friend, Pat, was excited about the idea, so we took this on together and planned our adventure.

In the home stretch Pat met someone, fell in love and changed her mind. I don't know where I found the gumption to go forward on my own, but I did. That choice took me to circumstances I never imagined.

Chapter Six

What's Before You Won't Pass You

CHAR AND STACY, also English nannies, were a welcome find in that thimble of a rural Pennsylvania community. Becoming fast friends, we orchestrated days off together—weekends in intriguing New York and trips to places that caught our fancy. Boringly straight-laced, I was in the company of liberated 'sixties' women that courted life with unfamiliar abandon. When the subject of their birth control pills came up, surprisingly, my eyes never betrayed my ignorance. *What exactly are birth control pills?* They assumed I knew. It must be an adult conversation and I was no adult; I was my mother's child. Free-spirited and easy going, my friends were always fun and adventurous. Hitched to them, I was along for an eye-widening ride.

My underpinning exclusively my mother: clinging to her skirts; reading her lines; acting out her production of my cloistered life; when I left home, I let go. Nothing even remotely prepared me for the real world outside her front door—a life unsecured and unmanageable without her. Minus her glue, the moral cocoon she intently spun defiantly split apart, dumping me defenseless into an unfamiliar, permissive society.

Together, Char and Stacy became my new mother—their skirts replaced hers; I followed where they led. On our way to a party at a prime university we snickered as I declared I would try out this curious thing called sex—I wanted to grow up, be like them. Prince Charming waited as if on cue.

There was no snickering on the way home as I recounted what happened. The trial run was a boring endeavor and too painful to complete—the parts didn't quite fit. In retrospect, I realize I'm lucky he listened when I told him I changed my mind. In retrospect, I was densely innocent and took no precautions. *What are precautions?* I never put sex and babies together. In over my head and drowning, the emancipation I imagined as sweet victory was, alas, a loss. I missed Mam's familiar constraints —without her, my life was on skids.

While still at home in England, taking the 2:00 a.m. last bus home from a weekend dance; I walked briskly in the middle of the road in edgy darkness from the bus stop to my house, relieved when the key turned successfully in the lock. I was eighteen. Waltzing in, I was tickled to see my mother. She waited up to make sure I was safe and sound. No one could make me feel safe and sound like her. I wanted *her* skirts again, not theirs.

The initial shock of emancipation faded and I gradually adapted; unfamiliar ways became familiar ones. I learned to let freedom be less daunting. I learned to survive and even to live without holding my mother's hand—as long as I had a surrogate. My work contract up, my horizons had definitely expanded, but I never truly grew up. I managed to stay the same skittish, immature girl I had always been.

Char and I shared a studio apartment in Phoenix, Arizona. Stacy lived with her boyfriend. Job hunting was tiresome, as potential employers, convinced I would relocate to California, were reluctant to take a chance on me. With only five dollars in my pocket, I landed a job as bookkeeper in a retail jewelry store. John, the manager, a French Canadian, prized the European work ethic and hired me based on that alone. He was divorced, with a steady girlfriend. His three sons lived with their mother.

Fifteen was school-leaving age in England. I stayed on until I was sixteen to take exams that would open doors to a better job, although no occupation especially interested me. My mother never told me what to be when I grew up. If she had, I would have been that. A representative from the Inland Revenue Service spoke to my class about work opportunities in income tax. When I passed the exams I was hired as a Tax Officer. Five years later, I left that job to travel to America. Arithmetic, not math, was required for tax work. I hoped the same was true of bookkeeping.

Public transportation in sprawling Phoenix was shabby. On weekends we rented a vehicle to get around, then, between us, we purchased a used car on credit. Char's job was on the bus route, mine was not, so I used the car for work.

We enrolled in night school to learn computer programming. School, rent and car payments took most of our money. I made minimum wage. Daily lunch was the same slice of yellow cheese on cheap, spongy white bread. Dinner was a jaded box of macaroni and cheese—a diet that led to ringworm.

Someone knocked on the front door—it was the middle of the night. I ignored it hoping the person would leave; the knocking continued. Standing cautiously by the door, in the sternest tone I could summon, I questioned who was knocking and why. The voice responded softly. His name was Lloyd; he was looking for Char. Whatever else he said, in a flash I was dressed and outside sitting next to him on the grass. *I must be demented—he is a complete stranger.*

Balmy air, palm fronds fanning the flighty breeze, magic scampering about, it was the perfect scene for seduction. He was, no kidding, drop dead gorgeous, and I was smitten. Char never mentioned him to me. *What on earth is she doing out somewhere when she has this magnificent creature in her life?*

Definitively, he was the proverbial tall, dark and handsome—randy blue eyes, luscious long lashes and a smile that no doubt captivated many women's hearts besides mine. Won over by his flirtatious charm, we talked until daybreak. I don't know how it happened, but when I walked him to his car we were holding hands.

My boss's relationship with his girlfriend ended when she quit her job at the store. Eventually, I gave in to John's invitations for dinners after work, unsure why he asked me in the first place. Perhaps he felt sorry for me with my dreary cheese sandwiches. Maybe he wanted company. I had zero romantic interest in him; he had demonstrated none in me. Dinners were a grand treat, however: great restaurants; fresh white tablecloths; attentive male waiters; and steaks, desserts, drinks dressed too pretty to disturb. He was fifteen years my senior, yet I never gave age a thought.

Lloyd and I kept our involvement secret until, somehow, Char found out. Perhaps I told her—perhaps not. For some reason Lloyd spent the night at our studio apartment. Char was not happy; uncharacteristic, unexpressed upset tightened her face. *I want to please both of them. What do I do? She's cross with me. I want her to like me. I should tell him to leave and I can't because I want him to like me, too. I'll just pretend everything's okay.*

If only she had chopped up the air with her anger—but she stewed instead. When romance enters the arena, sometimes sense flies out the window. Choosing a man I barely knew over a tried and true friend was an egregious, irreversible error and I would pay dearly for it.

I looked up from my desk at work: Char was at the counter, furious. She raised her voice just like my mother. I wanted to hide. When my mother shouted, whether or not I was to blame, I assumed I was. Zipped back to the past, I sat there mute. My mind flew off to its secret place. She held up her set of car keys, jingled them in front of her face and stormed out. All I remember of her tirade is that she was taking the car. I never saw her again.

That fast, I lost my friend, my transportation, and my home. Mam would have said, "You made your bed, now lay in it." Was that Catholic code for *pick up your cross and carry it?* I did not want a cross, thank you. I did not want a heartless beam digging into my shoulder ... but it was there anyway.

I must have phoned Stacy, although I don't remember it. I was at her fiancé's parents' house. They agreed that I could live with them in exchange for cleaning their house. The house was nice and I was grateful. However, I would not be living in their house as I assumed, but in the guest house. It was hidden at the far end of a narrow, lingering path—an add-on to the backside of the garage—a mere shed with plumbing and electricity.

Put off by the passage to find it, when I finally ferreted out the shed and walked in, I wanted to walk straight back out. I cried. *I have nowhere else to go. I can't believe I'm homeless. I can't believe I have to live here. Yesterday my life worked, now nothing makes sense. What am I going to do? I can't think straight. I don't even want to think.*

Ducking under lavish tree branches with their leaves brushing me, I walked hunched over in pitch darkness down the side of the garage and around the ghostly corner to finally reach the shed. I couldn't quickly rush inside and secure the door behind me, as there was no lock. Two exterior dirt-streaked, bare-faced windows enhanced the gloom of the place. The interior window across from the door faced the garage. A single bed lay under that naked window. In the silence of night, creaking tree branches scraped long fingernails against the brittle glass; all sorts of fear ran about as I tried to fall asleep. The homeowner's car headlights regularly burst from the garage, through the naked window into the blackened shed, lighting it up like Fourth of July fireworks, jolting me awake.

Lloyd showed up less often at my job and his calls at work dwindled from sparse to none. Increasingly impressed with John's business acumen, his wisdom, his uncanny ability to have the solution no matter the problem, I eventually assigned him the stature of Solomon. Down to earth, mature-minded, funny, he was easy to like. *I feel safe with him.* We slipped into unplanned sexual intimacy.

*

"You're pregnant." My mind wanted no part of it. It fled. Muddling empty-headed, if I was supposed to know what to do or say, I did not. Somebody needed to do something and I was not that somebody. The only action I could find was *reaction.*

Spontaneously processing out loud, peeking through rubble which two minutes earlier was me, whatever panicked thought popped into my head popped right out of my mouth. "What am I going to do? Do I have to have it?" The doctor sat at his desk scribbling, his eyes too busy to read mine. He only heard words. He didn't *see* me. His reply was laser. "Yes, you have to have it," he said.

"But I have no money," my panic darted back at him. Before I could digest the diagnosis, the solution was on his tongue. He knew attorneys. They had couples looking to adopt. They would pay the medical bills, and he would make the arrangements.

He took my words at face value responding to my ramblings. My emotions flew over his head. He was like my mother; tend to the physical symptoms and move on. He stepped over the heart in my words and his masculine head responded. He heard only a problem to be solved. He surely thought I didn't want my baby; I understand that now. *But we are talking about a life—two lives, not an ingrown toenail. I don't want a fix from his head. I want compassion from his heart. I need his validation and he is talking to me like a dismissed child.* He gave me the answer, what more did I want? *He's in charge.* Sadly, I was a child obeying the authority figure. I stopped talking out loud.

He did not explore other options with me, or even tell me there *were* other options; hand me leaflets or pamphlets to take with me to read when the stupor wore off; offer to talk it over; tell me to think about what he said and let him know; or send me to someone to help me sort it out. The deal was done. I didn't cry. I had been hit by a freight train. *I think I'm dead.*

I didn't remember leaving his office. I remembered, though, what I wanted to forget, *I'm pregnant and my baby belongs to somebody else.* The problem was not neatly put to bed as his prowess presumed. It was a nightmare that never slept. *I can't live this life. It can't be mine.*

Deferring to my mother and not standing up to her was costly. Consequently, I never learned to problem solve or trust that I could; when she wasn't there I located others who told me what to do, saved me, gave me answers. After all, others had minds that stayed put and figured things out. Mine did not. My father never actually said to me, "You're rubbish." Seeing the tasteless way he treated my mother, how she tolerated it, how she appeased him, I believed women were lesser beings than men. *Men are powerful. The doctor is powerful. I'm a woman. I am not.* That night John took me to see the movie, *Dr. Zhivago.* He didn't know I was pregnant. He thought the movie made me cry.

It seemed a thousand days passed before Lloyd, at last, phoned me at work. "I'm pregnant," I whispered, hoping no one overheard. His response, "Who's the father? You should tell him," kicked me in my gut. My mind ran off and I couldn't find a single word to speak. *Of course he's the father. I know it.* But his comment created uncertainty that never left. I was stuck with, *Is he the father, or is John*?

"I'm moving to California today, for good," he said. *He called to say goodbye.* I stopped listening to his empty words that bantered about like bothersome gnats. His was not the answer I expected. *What do I expect? I don't know. I thought that somehow everything would be alright if he knew. I never expected betrayal. I never thought he would reach for his running shoes.*

A million demons bit me with guilt. Sister Agnes's words, "It's always the girl's fault," clawed my skin. She warned me never to cross my legs; wear short skirts or use makeup—I did those things, and more. *The pregnancy is my doing—not his, not ours.* My mother's predictive phrases spat at me, "Men are no good. They only want one thing." There was nothing to say. I was stuck—an unwed mother—hung out to dry with hideous shame in a society intolerant of wanton women such as I, while he ran off unscathed.

*

John was unprepared for his initial walk, at night, down the snarly path to the shed, fumbling his way to find me. Fumbling, however, was the least of his surprises. As he stepped inside his mouth gaped open and did not close. His head shook from side-to-side as he sized up the rudimentary space that was my home. It seemed too much for him to process. Finally he spoke, "You can't stay here."

He soon found me a room to rent with a friendly family, bought me an old reliable purple Studebaker and gave me back my sense of freedom. By then he knew I was pregnant. He didn't tell anyone. He didn't have to. Time has a big mouth.

The rented room was as lonely as the shed. I could have joined the family in their living room to chat or watch television, but I didn't. Night after night I spent propped up on my bed, holding my belly, mimicking a protective mother hen sitting expectantly with her eggs—in reality, a prisoner on death row waiting for the inevitable, the death of separation. *Pregnant* flashed doggedly in my head like a persistent Las Vegas neon sign forcing itself through thin curtains into a seedy motel room window.

My mind tried to leave my predicament the way a battered woman tries to leave her abuser. Denial and fantasies my only scraps of peace, I ricocheted between them. *I'm not pregnant. I'll stay pregnant forever.* I believed them both. My mother always said, "What's before you won't pass you." I did not want what was before me. I banned it from my mind. I wanted something else. I wanted my life back. I wanted my dignity.

The urges to pee increased. A zillion treks to the bathroom would eventually arouse the family's suspicion. If they discerned I was pregnant, it could go either of two ways—I dreaded them both. They could be hostile and boot me out, for clearly I was a fallen woman, a fugitive from society hiding out in their home. Or they might be nice, compassionate. If they chose nice, I would crumble and cry, smashed like fragile glass into smithereens by reality—a million tiny shards impossible to piece back togeth-er—lost forever in a mind gone mad. *I need denial to keep reality at a distance to survive. Denial glues me together.*

Fortunately, there was an outside door to my room. I peed in my father's fancy pint-sized beer mug and dumped the urine on the grass. More and more imprisoned within my body, my room, my mind, my thoughts paced along a treacherous tightrope. Sometimes missing the soft landing of denial, they plunged in-stead into lurid loss.

John bought a home and I moved in with him; it seemed the next logical step. Materially speaking, I was rescued by my knight in shining armor, whisked away to his sumptuous castle.

Emotionally, I was thin skin stretched over bones. We cooked grand evening meals and sat together on the floor, backs against the couch, our food on the coffee table before us. Entertained by television rather than court jesters, like gluttonous guests at the banquet of King Henry V111, we were unconsciously lost in the oblivion of avoidance. Food was solace. I hoped it soothed my ba-by.

Desperate to conceal the stigma of shame, I purchased a girdle and wore it to work; within two hours I rushed home and tugged it off. I couldn't breathe and I was concerned it might hurt my ba-by. *Who am I trying to kid? My belly will be big and round and I will be humiliated.* Wanting to hide, instead, I was on display. As a child, I undressed in the dark or changed clothes standing inside a wardrobe that gave me the willies—a weirdness I would rather have side-stepped than stepped into—because I did not want God to see me naked, and God sees all. With a pregnant belly, there was nowhere to hide—except in my head.

Why couldn't I be guilty of a minor sin such as shoplifting a lipstick? That would not have blown up my belly for the world to see and condemn. And a pissed-off God would not punish me by wrenching away my child. I depended on the oxygen of approval to survive. *How will I survive without it? I can't be pregnant—I'm good.* I became the opposite of who I wanted to be. I became the poster girl for immorality.

Co-workers looked through me with glass eyes, eerily mimicking my family of origin, pretending out loud that all was well. *What pregnancy?* No one commented on my belly because none, including me, dared speak the truth, except Julie. She had guts enough to see my belly and volunteered her mother, whom I had never met, to make me maternity clothes: two dresses, one pink and one green. I rotated them like uniforms: pink one day, green the next.

Julie and I didn't talk beyond the dresses. Talking about my circumstance made it real. *I can't be with real. Pregnant and goodbye are inseparable. I cannot be with one without the other.* If I had to shop for maternity clothes, be that present to being pregnant, that present to my baby leaving me, my heart would burst right out of my chest. *How did I become so tainted so quickly?*

Pretending at work became easier until customers commented on my condition or asked incisive questions. If I was quick with a generic quip that shut them up, I was home free. If I failed and the truth was obvious, everyone fell silent holding our collective breath, processing embarrassment, judgment, or both. It galled me to take on their representation of who I was. *I can't bear to be the pariah others see when they see me. I am not that, but to them my belly says otherwise.* Connecting with reality was cruel pain I ditched at every opportunity.

My belly was large and I was emaciated, starved for approval. My belly defined me. People in my life closed their hearts based on a belly that stopped them in their tracks. They forgot I was a human being. I became someone to keep at a distance for they could be sullied by association. Perhaps they were afraid I might rub off on them. Society's unfair, immoral view of me was insurmountable and inescapable. I too became the hostage of its hype, simultaneously believing it and battling it. *The force of their condemnation smothers me like thick fog . . . I can't see my way forward. There is no way out. They want me to die for my sin. Do they know they have won? I am emotionally eaten alive, dying quietly, slowly, and it's not quick enough for me or them.* Denial, my faithful companion, kept me sane and alive.

True consolation came from my innocent baby. Supposed to be the comforter, instead my baby comforted me. The tiny heel caressed back and forth along my side. I cradled my hand around it as it moved. Time stopped. It was just us two, in the moment, loving each other.

John told me he couldn't handle small children, they made him nervous. He didn't want my baby, any baby for that matter. I was attached to John: psychologically dependent on him. He was the only person that physically stood by me in my pregnancy. I relied on him. I loved him and wanted to please him. John was the only person permitted to see my suffering, and he was emotionally unavailable to me. In a very real sense he was infected with society's virus—it killed off his compassion. He too saw only a belly and a belly was bad.

John ignored my tears and my pleas to keep my baby. When I lost control and begged, he continued on with whatever he was doing, or found something else to do, effectively stonewalling me. His eyes avoided mine, his reply remained unchanged, "I don't want any more kids."

We got no further than that. We didn't talk in depth about the pregnancy or anything else. When I wanted and needed his acceptance and support the most, when I believed it was crucial in keeping my baby, he kept it to himself. I didn't give up on going to him in tears, however, just one more time. He wouldn't let me in. I firmly believed that in the final moment, John would not abandon me. *He will come around. He has to.*

It was Christmas Eve. I phoned my mother in England and pinched my finger until it hurt to keep from crying. Hearing her voice then so darling, so dear, my heart quivered in my throat. I wanted more than anything to tell her I was pregnant.

I flashed back to my later teens when life had much improved: mailbags came home filled with tossed salad fixings, a yummy onion sauce to pour over potatoes, brown bread, and more. A pot of Irish stew with meat and fresh vegetables would be simmering on the stove. There was less fighting then. At seventeen, working late, cold, dark and wintry outside, I called home to see what was for tea. The dish she mentioned was not pleasing, yet the caring in her voice was bliss.

Talking to her now, I pictured the tan and white cardigan she often wore, a sharp contrast to her bossy all-the-time uniform. Her attitude had softened greatly, perhaps the result of more grown-up children and less responsibility. She could have been my salvation. Secretly I hoped for that. Yet I could not speak the words. I had become the corrupt girl, shamed the name she struggled to keep decent.

My father was dead. My mother still wrestled to make ends meet. Any notion of sending my child home to my mother or going home with my child was desperate and fanciful—a pipe dream at best. Shame, my master, would never allow it.

With all avenues blocked and no safe haven, my options stayed the same for me and my unborn child: death and death. Death if we stayed together; *How could we survive*? My home and job linked to John, I presumed I would have neither if I kept my baby. The social stigma was callous. *Where would we go? Who would help us? Who would mind my baby while I look for work, go to work? How could I get enough money for us to live, to pay a babysitter?* With no allies then, how would we magically find willing hearts and hands later? I hated reality; it was full of questions with no answers. And there was death if we parted; *How can I live without my child?*

I never really believed I had the option to keep my baby—that was the root of my suffering—the true torture of the reality with which I was dealing. Reality itself was a death sentence. I fell once again into denial as there was no big picture, no future. I couldn't look ahead and picture myself with a baby, nor could I picture my baby in someone else's arms. My mind couldn't forge past the prognosis of adoption.

In a very real way, I sentenced myself that day in the doctor's office. Without my lips moving, I promised my baby to someone else. I needed permission to keep my baby. I didn't get it from the doctor, and I couldn't give it to myself. The doctor's humanism would have been as sweet as a priest's benediction. Instead, our words, rather the lack of them, drew a box outside of which I could not escape. With blind trust, I gave others the responsibility to decide for me, and the results were hellish. Doing what I thought was the only thing I could do—nothing—I waited with dread for a departure I couldn't bear. *There is nothing I can do. I am powerless to change the inevitable. I have been shoveled into adoption.*

Chapter Seven

The Execution

WITHOUT WARNING, warm water rushed down my legs. I was standing by the bed when it happened. Electrified, I could not move. Fantasies I let steal my mind left me utterly unprepared to deal with the attrition that day expected to exact. An illusory day—it was never supposed to come. *I should know what to do. She always did. I should be able to cope. She did. I should be strong. She was.* Wishing I had my mother's spirit, I wasn't even close. She was a superwoman; me, a mere victim.

True to her Irish Catholic faith, my mother lived martyrdom. Suffering, the more the better, was God's way of letting her get close to Him. She bargained her much-loved fish and chips for years, in exchange for a miraculous turnaround in David's behavior. What she got, however, was more suffering. "Every day you must take up your cross and carry it; the heavier the cross, the greater the crown." Her gospel; she recited it, she lived it.

That day especially, the cross I rebuked was there to nail my heart. It never entered my mind to haggle with God—I had no bargaining rights. *I am bad—who am I to pray?* I did not repent, say I was sorry, beg for forgiveness, or make panicked promises. I purposely dodged God, unplugging from a power that pinned up a wanted poster with my picture, hoping He would forget about me, although I knew better. There was no cloak of clemency, no sanctuary within the church for me, and no reprieve from society.

Suffer, go without. Offer it up for your sins. That's what I was taught and what I lived. I thought I was supposed to suffer for others, do what others wanted; give me up for them, and I did that. I suffered. *Do penance, it's lent. Make the sacrifice, go to mass and Holy Communion on the first Friday of the month, for nine consecutive months, and you will die in God's favor and escape hell. Suffer to avoid suffering. What?? Shut up, be good and you will be rewarded. Where's the reward? Oh, you'll get it when you die.* I had swallowed the same bitter pill she did.

I thought that when I died, I would sit on a throne in heaven, in the presence of God: finally protected from all harm, finally safe, finally loved for me, as I am. At least I could look forward to that in my piss poor, scary childhood and life. Being good was an investment in me. At least there was a happy ending somewhere, a grand pay-off, even if I had to wait for it until I was old and worn down. It was better than money, better than stuff. Believing that, was the unconscious mechanism that ran me. *Atone, Atone, Atone … And now you want my child!!!*

Transported by my mind to my childhood bedroom, I knelt beside my bed at the altar: a small table topped with a white doily splashed with prayer book-sized, colorful, holy pictures of saints. I prayed—never directly to God, that was too scary—to the Virgin Mary and the saints to intervene on my behalf. *What happened to that girl? Who have I become?*

The phone conversation with John was brief. He was at work; it was my day off. Not offering to take me to the hospital, he asked if I was going. *I don't want to go to that place.* Why would anyone step out of complicity with society to step up for me? Yet that's what I had hoped for—at least from John. No one to run to, no one to hold my hand, nowhere else to go and in labor, I drove myself to the hospital. Actually, my car took me there. It just looked as if I was driving.

Hell was a white hospital room; walls, ceiling, linens, and staff all crisply coalesced into a barren kind of iciness. Drab, drawn drapes choked off outside life. I felt dirty in that pristine place. John was on the phone. Useless scraps of words shuffled between us; mostly he held on while I winced in pain. I wanted to tell him I was in hell, beg him to save me. I wanted to tell him I was all alone in that sorry room and the pain was awful. I wanted to tell him I didn't know how to have a baby and I was scared. But I didn't. There was no point.

Hell's fire raged in my body. White-hot pokers seared my insides. Intermittently, a nurse, chilly and well-suited to her surroundings, bobbed in and out of the space. She did not come to my bedside or speak one word until I begged for something for the pain. "No. It's too soon," she said and left.

What does 'too soon' mean? I hurt now. What is happening to my body? Somebody help me. Locked in labor's intense grip and helpless, I was at the mercy of one that clearly had none. The family dog getting her nails clipped would have engendered more benevolence. No one asked how I was or what I needed. No kind-eyed souls, no gentle pats of reassurance, no calming smiles—just ghost-dressed, calloused shadows in the background of my personal nightmare.

I wanted my mother. She would have sorted them out with a few stiff syllables. She would have saved me. I wanted to wriggle off the bed and run, but my body betrayed me. It was in too much pain to move. Thoughts of escape conjured up by panic were dead-end streets, delusions. Our time together had run out. Like a nail on the finger of my body, my baby slowly ripped away in waves of blazing pain. *Don't leave me, not you too. How can my body do this to me?*

My familiar-faced gynecologist would have brought some reassurance. In his place, however, a mute, masked stranger stood at the foot of my bed—long, silver tongs screamed in his fist. Fear jumped on me in layers. *What kind of torture is next?* A sneaky, secret needle stabbed me into oblivion.

*

I woke up in a different room; the pain was different. My baby was gone. *Where am I? Why was I asleep? What did they do to me?* No one told me I would be unconscious for my baby's birth. No one said my baby would vanish. No more than a convicted criminal, I had no say. Invalidated as a feeling human being, a mother and contributor to my own child's birth, my baby was consequently born alone into an antiseptic environment with self-righteous strangers more morally laced than tightly-tied sneakers.

One moment the doctor said I was pregnant, and with his next breath my baby belonged to a respectable couple: a dad, a stay-at-home mom in a lovely house, a nice nursery stuffed with cuddly toys, and walks in the park in a bouncy new pram. Just where did love fit into that socially acceptable future? Innately, I knew how to perfectly love my own baby and if maternal love was paramount instead of condemned, we had what we needed.

Nothing in me wanted my baby to leave and I could not resolve that outcome within myself. To keep my baby simply because I cherished my child more than I could have dreamed possible, seemed selfish. Everything in me, including my heart, wanted to be selfish, even as it sank into submission to a societal moray whose elusive heart I could not find. I wanted to plead for mercy. I wanted my baby. I wanted my baby to have me. *How dare they?* A vacant mound sat on my belly where my baby used to be. *Or did it? Perhaps it was just a dream. I probably made the whole thing up. I didn't give birth; I never saw a baby.*

Still an outcast, still in the embargo of silence and afraid to ask, I asked anyway, "What did I have?" The nurse whisking by in a blur did not look at me as I spoke.

"A girl," she said curtly, no break in her stride.

Nurses are not supposed to robotically bandage wounds. When they saw me, however, they bandaged their hearts. They're supposed to care. I thought caring was a prerequisite for their profession, obviously not—not when you're an unwed mother. Their careless contempt, their silent treatment, was ridiculously childish and effectively condemning.

A pair of them took a spot on either side of the bed. Together they massaged my empty belly, bantering back and forth across my body in mindless manipulation of a stomach that appalled them. Every time they massaged my belly warm blood whooshed out. It did not phase them—it never broke their code of silence or shifted their gaze to me. *Why don't they tell me what's going on? Why is there so much blood? Why doesn't it stop? I could bleed to death and no one would know. No one would care, including me. I am, after all, a boil on society, an inferior nobody who deserves death for giving birth.* I was not cautioned to ask for assistance getting out of bed. I took a few steps, and fainted.

A woman's mouth beside a male suit, took me by surprise; someone was talking to me, or more accurately, at me. "Your baby is just perfect. She has big blue eyes and dark hair," the mouth blitzed, unconcerned for my attacked heart and my fractured state of mind. The suit said nothing.

I have a child? Where is she? How dare you make her real when she's gone? How dare you tell me how lovely my child is! What kind of punishment is this, anyway? Confident, alert, primped, they were gussied up with dominance, armored against me at my weakest. I stood with them at the door, the pathetic opponent that I was: barefoot, disheveled, gripping a gaping hospital gown to stay modest, doused in shame and standing shell-shocked without back-up.

Of course I looked pathetic! I just had a baby who was never mine. She just vanished. I was stuck with stone-eyed, frozen-hearted nurses that denied my existence (even that I had had a baby) and a manic mind yelling *I can't stand this! It's not happening. I just can't stand this*, until deafness drowned my ears.

My insides twisted into tight braids. I wanted to vomit, and rockets exploded in my brain, all while she gratingly chattered on like fingernails scraping a blackboard, *but not a word about the paper she handed me.* She wanted my signature on the paper, utterly oblivious to my life destructing before her eyes. Dutifully, a compliant child wrote with my adult hand my name on a paper I was without competence to read, let alone comprehend. I wanted to escape. I wanted them out of there. Still babbling, the mouth left with the suit.

My legs dropped me face down on the bed. I was dead—I had to be. My heart could not hold that much pain. Sorrow burst out everywhere. Hysteria shot from every atom in me. My body shook uncontrollably in the aftermath of unimaginable, indescribable loss—nine months of stashed agony whooshed out like blood. Tears streamed from my eyes, mouth and nose. A blurry uniform dared offer something to calm me, intruding on grief impossible to interrupt.

Inside a body that could not stop itself from trembling and whimpering, I lay defeated in my own battlefield, mourning death, grieving a mortal wound—alone at a funeral no one cared took place.

The uniform came back, "It will look good on your chart if I give you a sedative. The other nurses may stop ignoring you." I took the pill because sadness could not bear to leave me and I could not stand the sorrow. I took it to escape from hell.

There were no phone calls or visitors, no flowers, cards, or acknowledgements of any kind. Back to wondering, *Did I really give birth? If I did, where is my baby?* I tried to put a face of sense on what seemed like madness. *Am I in a mental institution: delusional, already insane? I thought I had a baby.* I was afraid to think. *If my baby is really here, I could never leave.* And thus my mixed-up mind coped without her until my ten-day sentence in the hospital ended.

The hemorrhoids were heartless. I stopped eating for days to avoid the agony of evacuation. I wanted to physically die. Emotionally, I already had. Why couldn't it be a condition socially acceptable to discuss, rather than an embarrassing keep-under-wraps one?

A week later, John made an appointment for me with his doctor. How I managed to get myself out of bed or dressed was beyond me. A corpse gasped back from the mirror startling us both. Holding the railing I pulled myself up the stairs from the lower level, shuffled to the front door and to the car to drive myself.

Mere steps from the parking lot to the doctor's office seemed a marathon trek. A patient driver waited as I crossed. She leaned on the steering wheel gazing inquisitively at a misshapen, ashen young woman making her worn-out journey: bent over, legs bowed, every step slow and precise.

Ordinarily, humiliation would have crushed me. Spent, defeated, exhausted, I did not give a damn. Every expanded eye in the waiting room perched itself on me. I imagine they had never seen such a bleached face on a living soul, or such a youthful woman ambling along like an octogenarian with arthritic legs, painstakingly plotting her steps across the floor as though it were a minefield. That, by the way, was the only time I've bypassed the waiting room and been taken directly to see the doctor.

"What happened to you?" Concerned words from a considerate face caught me off guard. Somebody actually cared about me. I began to cry. "It's okay," he hushed, "Take your time."

"I just had a baby." The words limped out between sobs.

"Were there any complications?" he asked.

A huge complication, I don't have her. I lied, "She was stillborn."

There was no way to account for her absence except to lie, and I was starving for kindness. If I told the truth he would let me suffer, as that seemed to have been the medical protocol. After the examination, he comfortingly patted my arm. "You have less than half the blood you're supposed to have in your body. We'll start with blood transfusions." As it turned out, I ended up in the hospital for surgery.

Back on my feet, I promptly went to the lawyer's office. With more dignity about me—no gaping hospital gown, no bare feet, no crazed futility cramming fat fingers in my ears, no fatigue from hemorrhaging—I was as clear-minded as a new mother minus her child could be. Both scared and confident, I took a stand for my baby, reneging on an adoption deal I did not want in the first place—a deal forged from fear and desperation.

"Can I help you?" a woman asked.

"Yes," I answered. "Three weeks ago I had a baby girl." I told her my name. "Your office handled the adoption. I want my baby back."

Phew! It was over. Without my baby, I was emotionally wasted. Without her, there was no life. She was mine and I was hers. We belonged together. John is a good man. When he saw an actual living breathing baby girl in my arms, not a bump on my belly, his heart had to melt. He loved me, surely he would love her. He would never turn us away. He was not that kind of man. We would make it work. *I want my baby!*

Casually the middle-aged woman stood up, took off her glasses and put them carefully on the desk. My eyes locked on hers. My stomach hurt. "I'm afraid that's not possible."

She offered a fake smile. *What did she say?* "I can make a call to the family that adopted her to see how she is." Something unknown to me nodded my head in agreement. She left the room to make the call. I did not move or process a single thing while she was gone. How could I, my mind went missing. When she stepped back into the room she smiled. "The baby is just fine," she said.

My baby is never coming back to me. Drenched in emotions I had no idea how to handle, who held me up? What pinned my sanity together? Right there and then I should have gone mad and been done with it. *She's mine. They know I want her. Why are they keeping her from me?* No one told me the rules. The mouth never said I could not have her back. She never told me specifically what I was signing or if I signed, that it was forever. *Why didn't she explain what adoption means? My baby is not like Tina, she's not eligible for adoption! She's not an orphan! She has a mother! She has me!*

My baby was with the adoptive family less than thirty days. I could return a sweater in the same amount of time and undo the transaction. Why not a baby? If it were a dog whose owner showed up puppy-eyed to claim it, they would give it back. *Why won't they give a baby back to a mother who didn't want to lose her in the first place? How can they turn their backs on me like this? I could explain if they'd just let me. But why should I have to, she's my baby! How can anyone deny me my own child?*

I found courage too late. Legally she was not mine: morally and maternally, she was, is, and always will be. I was alive, as the dull knife hacked around my heart and carelessly gouged it from my body. Because I was an unwed mother, no one cared. No one wanted to deal with the messy feelings of a woman who did not matter. Invisible pallbearers carried me down the stairs from the office and dumped my remains into a grayness that simulated existence. That I survived and stayed sane is remarkable.

Chapter Eight

Dead or Alive, Life Moves On

THE MORTAL WOUND killed me. I should have died but my body breathed itself into fake aliveness and I walked among the living, in a dead woman's shoes. All depths, layers and levels that once were me shriveled like a popped balloon hanging lifeless from the ceiling by a tawdry thumb tack. My heart seeks *always*. It tempts my mind and tries to find a route within me back to what once was me but now is gone. The air knows my sadness. Flowers have lost their prettiness, clouds are mourning cloaks, and birds sing taps. She is gone. I put on make-up—but she is gone. I go to work—but she is gone. I am a mother with no arms: a mother without maternal power. I am a mother without her child.

Who pulled me out of bed, dressed me, painted my face, and mechanically pushed me through daily routines so ordinary that I was hypnotized into believing the previous nine months were no more than an abstract dream? Who orchestrated the continued conspiracy of co-workers so that no one mentioned a baby, a birth or a belly bargained away? And so the play of *pretend* resumed, picked up where it left off—a game never interrupted.

My mind's magic machinery handling life-ending loss that I could not, allowed me to flat-line through life, inexplicably functioning without feeling. As long as my emotions were anesthetized, securely separated from the memory of her, an indecipherable detouring in my brain, she was safe, at least in my head. I searched faces of babies, querying mothers about birth dates. I was particularly preoccupied with her on her birthday and Mother's

Day; on days when thoughts of her triggered her so electrically to me I could think of nothing else; on days when my own gut hurt because I felt or feared that *she* hurt; on days that I cried and asked the Virgin Mary to protect her. Strangely enough, her ghost heel still stroked slowly back and forth along my side as if she never left. I was grateful for it, it was comforting.

Based on my experience, I believe no woman initially of sound mind can dutifully, out of desperation or under duress, give up a child that grew in her belly, her heart, her psyche, and survive the loss intact. We lose some*thing*—some*thing* words can't touch, some*thing* non-physical. Such separation of a mother from her child contradicts nature. Even animals are permitted to lick and love their young at birth and instinctively nest. Society's tall finger standing against the pressed lips of adoption can never shush away the innate bond of a mother with her child. Without my baby, something intrinsic to my very being perished. My Spirit, ripped in half, yearned for its missing piece. Nothing else could complete it.

Nine months after her birth, I married John in an impromptu stark ceremony in a Las Vegas wedding chapel. John became acquainted with a Pastor, whose presumed credibility caught an ordinarily savvy John off-guard. John resigned from the jewelry store, withdrew his profit-sharing money, and with it bought acreage from the Pastor. He took a job at another jewelry store and worked really long hours. I worked two jobs as John had substantial child support, alimony and an ex-marital debt to pay. We scrimped without worrying, positive our financial future was secure as the result of our land investment.

John's uncle, a Catholic priest and brilliantly shrewd man who transcribed holy books into various languages, offered to front him money to open his own store. John was a sure bet to succeed, an expert in his inherited field—you could say jewelry decorated his genes. He took on a partner, but when the partner baled I quit my jobs; replaced him; and trailed along, protected in John's shadow.

Predictably, John did things his way. Even so, we fought infrequently because we dodged issues and lived emotionally stingy lives. When we fought, he brought up where he found me, down and out in the shed, insinuating I was in his debt. I knew I owed him. I loved him. It was easy to stay.

John's three boys were ages three to thirteen. John was not wired with an instinctual nurturing for young children. I felt resigned to a life without our own kids. Whenever I mentioned a baby, his sons appeared as if by magic—his way of keeping maternal urges in check. Any notion that I may have wanted a child, if there on Friday, disappeared by Sunday evening when John packed the boys into his car after their weekend stay to return them to their mother. No. I did not want a child, at least not a boy. I shuddered at the very thought. "How do you feel about having a baby now?" he teased.

"No way," I shot back. We laughed. He poured his glass of red wine, and I sank into the security of the armchair, both of us recuperating from their turbulent visit.

One day his youngest child, still innocent, cuddled close on my knee. "Mommy said Daddy doesn't live with us because you have him."

Prickled by his unexpected words, I was more annoyed by what he was told, and how it colored him against me. Kissing his head I whispered, "You miss your Daddy?"

"Yes," he said. "I want him to live at my house. Mommy said you won't let him. Why won't you let Daddy come home?"

Obviously, the loving connection I enjoyed with the little one was over. I took my heart back and hid it once again. I was the same enemy to him I was to his brothers. If it were not for me, their dad would be with their mother, or so they thought. They resented me, stuck me in the role of wicked stepmother and I saw no way out. They judged me as *bad* before they even knew me. Lacking maturity to do otherwise, I cut all emotional ties to them with sharp scissors and merely tolerated them. The contempt between us was mutual. That steamy second, I wanted my own child.

I stopped using birth control. John would never have understood why. He would have been bent on talking me out of it. The consequences of not telling him, however, never occurred to me. Although I had given no prior serious thought to having another baby, suddenly I longed to be a mother holding my own flesh and blood, loving a child who could love me back, a child I could keep. *I am not waiting for permission. It's time, because I say it is. And, I do not just want a baby. I want a girl.* Right then and there I mentally created her. I never doubted it would play out otherwise. I just knew I would have a girl.

I basically tricked John into fatherhood. He did not like children, couldn't relate to them and only enjoyed them when they were older. *Blah, blah, blah.* I knew all that but it didn't deter me. The past, however, managed to creep in and I began to fear the natural excitement of getting pregnant. My mother ended up being with us from England for an extended stay. During that time, I learned to initiate affection with her and she eagerly loved me back. Perhaps subconsciously I felt safe getting pregnant knowing she would protect my baby and me.

John was focused at his jeweler's bench when I walked into the store, much like walking a pirate's plank, mentally debating whether to tell him then or wait for the elusive, perfect moment. He looked up, put down his tools, and asked what was wrong. Cornered, I hesitated, wondering exactly how to phrase it. The words rushed out before I had a chance to neatly arrange them. "I just came from the doctor's office. I'm pregnant. Can I keep it?" *I'm so stupid. Why did I say that? Neither heaven nor earth is going to take this baby from me. Regardless of his reaction I am keeping my baby.* In the eyes of the Catholic Church we lived in sin. Regardless of God's wrath *I am keeping my baby. And I will be wide awake for the birth.*

He jumped to his feet smiling. "Of course," his voice was excited. I cried and laughed—tears for my first child, joy for my second. Would a second child hush the loss of the first? My doctor knew having a girl was vital. Coaxing my long-awaited child from my body, a smile squinted around his eyes. "It's a girl," he announced. John and I had been married for five years.

*

She was perfect. She was beautiful. Finally, a mother holding her longed-for child, I was blissfully happy, yet devastatingly depressed and constantly crying. My mother assured me such feelings were natural after giving birth. She was right—and she didn't know then about my first child. Jacqueline's birth was supposed to have lulled that loss: eased the pain, which instead, exploded.

I was pregnant with Jacqueline when we learned the land purchase was a scam. A second mortgage on our home was attached to that purchase. Unwilling to throw good money after bad, John doggedly refused to pay the second mortgage. Jacqueline was two weeks old when we were evicted. We lost the land we thought we owned, our money, and our home. No sooner had we moved into a rented house than John suffered a stroke and lost his peripheral vision. Actually, he was lucky to be alive. Before long, we saved up the down payment for a ranch style home, settled back into some semblance of a normal family life and paid back his uncle.

The ghost of my first child, however, began to shadow the life of my second. I wanted them both: my two babies. When Jacqueline awoke during the night, my mother and I fought over who would tend to her. I wanted her all to myself. Without question, John adored Jacqueline. He held her, played with her, but was clueless how to help with any other baby-related tasks. When I complained to him, he complained back; between me and my mother he could not get a look in. He was right. I trusted my mother wholeheartedly and still I guarded Jacqueline like a mother bird nervously walking the beat of her nest.

My mother worked with us at the store, and Jacqueline came along too. She never had a babysitter other than my mother and usually, wherever John and I went, so did they. Over-protective from the moment she was born, I knew I could not lose her to anyone, for any reason, but the past insisted that I could. Neither my heart nor my mind would survive such devastation a second time.

Eventually, my mother returned to England and I took on the exclusive care of Jacqueline, which took more of my time. The effervescence of her birth fizzled out and John remembered his discomfort with children. He said I neglected him in favor of her, that things had changed between us and I was too busy for him. Jacqueline was my life. John came second. He knew it. I denied it.

In a sense, John and I were like kids emotionally stunted during dysfunctional childhoods. Intimate communication was not something we knew how to do. We carried our wounds with us. They were raw and we had no ointment to heal them.

When Jacqueline was a toddler, John became more actively involved. They both beamed when she crawled up on his knee in the evenings for their own special ritual, and she pretended to puff on his aromatic pipe. There was never a question he loved her. He did, immensely; he just was unable to demonstrate it. Maybe his role models were as emotionally bereft as mine. His time in the loveless orphanage with stringent nuns no doubt played its part. As Jacqueline got older John was more involved, more comfortable, finally a dad, and their relationship blossomed into something beautiful.

John's long-lost and vaguely-remembered cousin paid a surprise and opportune visit. He spoke openly about something called *meditation* and connecting with a *Divine* presence within. Meditation had saved his life during a time when he had nothing left to live for. *A Divine being within someone like me?* That was the most amazing thing I had ever heard. Raised in a worm-of-the-dust mentality—born behind the eight ball so to speak—no matter what I did, I would never be good enough for God's nod.

More than ready for a more pleasing perspective, I began to practice meditation. John called it hocus pocus and said I was nuts! It did not end there. We raised chickens for eggs, sheep, goats and a cow. Ready to be eaten, all but the chickens were collected by the butcher who dressed and returned them in neat white paper packages that fattened the freezer. Winnie, a wonderfully docile woolly sheep lay on my plate reduced to a lamb chop; I could not eat her in spite of John's manipulation. Customary, inhumane butchery practices caught my attention. Not wanting to contribute to animal suffering, I stopped eating meat.

John wanted me to change back to more familiar ways, but I could not. The more I delved into searching for my *Self* through meditation and reading books, the more seeking lured me, and the more dissatisfied I became with life as I lived it.

I got up before John and Jacqueline and faithfully practiced yoga from a book I found at the health food store. Yoga gave me a sense of well-being, a sense of peace. It gave me a sense of inner courage, an inexplicable feeling of preparing for battle. The discipline of yoga taught me that holding challenging poses transfers to courageously facing life challenges, as opposed to pushing against them, running from them, or pretending they don't exist. I learned about ways to be that I was not, ways to which I aspired.

I took up jogging in serene neighborhoods before life en masse erupted into bustling activity, until a car stalked and spooked me into stopping my routine. Angry with myself for being afraid, I decided to learn karate. Too intimidated to go alone, I took Jacqueline, rationalizing it would be good for her, and it was.

Me of all people, an active participant in karate; punching, kicking, sparring, I dragged my beat-up body out of bed morning after achy morning. Bruised, bones fractured, smacked down, I always went back for more, more, more. As a slender, timid female, karate was my most unlikely bedfellow. Worth every *ouch* of physical pain, it gave me a sense of liberation and power, as if my inner warrior was awakening.

Before long I taught kids at the Dojo. At night, at home, I practiced karate while John watched television. *Has karate slipped in to widen even more the gap between us?* Whatever it took to avoid problems, I did. I stuffed things inside, pretended they didn't exist, ran from them, anything to bypass, rather than rouse, confrontation. *Don't rock the boat and keep the peace* were my survival tools. They were the tools I had mastered.

Attempts at assertiveness failed with John. Whenever I spoke up I lost, suffering through days of silent treatment until I couldn't stand it, then babied him back into communication, faulty as it was.

The first robbery at the store was terrifying. Forcibly flanked side-by-side on the floor under the snout of a shotgun, three of us as victims lessened the awfulness because it was shared.

The second time, robbers entered by night through the roof.

The third time was the worst; alone in the store, two gunmen, one male and one female, held me at gunpoint. The front door was electronically locked. My life flashed like lighting through my mind. Imperceptible to them, I triggered the silent alarm. Lo and behold, the new cash register opened without the customary fuss. I unlocked without incident all the showcases as directed, watched them steal our merchandise, rifle through my purse, and through the vault—and it galled me to stand there violated, powerless.

A police officer rapped on the door, then disappeared. Visibly rattled, the couple did not speak; fear lasered between their eyes. Twice I suggested they go out the back way. *Just go! Please just go! Get out!* They did not respond.

In charge, the male instructed his partner to take me into the small bathroom. Her adrenaline was pumping; so was mine. In those close quarters, with the gun pointed at my head I debated tackling her, *but what then? What about him?*

As I contemplated my next move the male ordered us out of the bathroom. He told me to lie down on the floor. If I obeyed, I knew I was dead, for that's how it panned out in another store's recent robbery. I preferred to take my chances standing. I looked at him inches from my face and did not move. Distracted, he seemed to be weighing his next step. "Is there a back door?" he asked.

Incredibly, the railroad tie usually used as a barricade was off the door and the fiddle-some lock opened with the first attempt. They did not spy the waiting police officers and darted out with their loot. With the door secured behind them, I ran through the store and out the front door, three doors down to the safety of the barber shop, and burst inside. When I opened my mouth to tell my tale I could not speak. I wanted to get the fear out of me by telling them, but annoyingly, I was mute. A barber at last asked, "Did you get robbed?" I nodded yes.

Absolute amazement that I managed sufficient outer calm to meet the robbers' demands did little to diminish my fear. For years afterwards, everywhere I went I was scared out of my wits: public bathrooms, empty hallways, confined spaces, parking lots, even at home. Being in the store was intolerably anxiety-producing. I suspected every male that walked in had a hidden gun, and women could not be trusted either.

Customers came into the store; I went outside until they left. I worked in a fishbowl for thieves and I wanted out. I told John I was too scared to work there anymore. I would get a job somewhere else. He needs me here, he said. *I can't leave.* Trapped, I stayed there, scared stiff.

We built a home and filled it with brand new furniture. All the *material* things I wanted, I had. But by the time I realized it was there—the vacuum in my *being*, the hole in my *self*—it was too late. Desperate to fill it, I crammed things into the void to feel full until mere things lost their luster. I could have had orange crates for furniture and not cared. *I never planned on this emptiness. I don't want it. It just happened somehow, and now it won't go away.* I wanted to want the house. I wanted to want my life. It was then that I stopped being happy.

Diving into meditation and spirituality, the more I learned, the hungrier I became for more knowledge and inspiration. I made the mistake of righteously foisting my new beliefs on John, which only caused arguments. My learnings were gibberish to him. He did not want to surrender his Catholic faith or believe that heaven is a state of mind rather than the payoff for a struggled, sacrificed life. As for vegetarianism, he could not embrace that either. Neither would he try. Stubbornly, he dug in his heels. He began cooking meat for his *own* dinner.

Our lifestyles created a fork in the road of our relationship. He was content in his comfortably entrenched ways. I was swept towards a desire for wholeness by a momentum I could not resist. There was nothing to talk about except work. I had had my fill of working at the store and talking about the store. Stretched further and further apart, we had less and less in common. My debt had been paid; we were even.

Chapter Nine

Change Is Inevitable

TREADING TEPIDLY to not tip the boat, I capsized it. Taking every ounce of moxie I could mush together I marched out the door of my marriage after fifteen years. Our relationship was built on unresolved issues—hexed from the start. *Feelings, what are those? Intimacy—you mean sex, don't you?* Emotionally miles apart, the repressed anger, resentment and grief over the loss of my child, had subconsciously walled her in the crevasse that grew between us.

I cried and cried, then cried some more. No matter where I was or who I was with, tears fell, until one day they did not. Jacqueline wanted to go back to her nice house, her own bed and a life she loved. My explanations made no sense to her—her questions never stopped. And the endless, daily decisions I had to make alone, made me want to scream. I was afraid to choose, afraid to make the wrong choice. Single motherhood was scary and intimidating.

I worked at an office job where I cried too much, stared off into space too much, and made too many mistakes. I was fired—the first time ever. Trying to wrap my brain around being sacked and accusations of errors I was convinced I never made, I went back to my desk and continued to work. *How am I supposed to know being fired means tools down and leave now, this minute?* I felt stupid.

Another office job in a furniture plant popped up with a boss who was thrilled with my work, until we crossed swords. One day, without warning, he told me to work by myself in the furniture outlet store. Still shadowed by the jewelry store robberies, fear piped right up and I said, "No." Had my mind not scampered off, I would have thought to give an explanation rather than an abrupt, insubordinate no. Eyebrows lifted. My co-worker put her head down and pretended to be busy. Used to unquestioning obedience, my boss was not a man to mess with. Still, no threat would send me to work in a retail store. My co-worker was right, retaliation followed. He would show me, and reassure his employees that he wore the boots.

Rentals an aside venture, he sent me to meet a potential male renter in a rough neighborhood at a hovel that was supposed to be a house. I did not want to get out of my car, never mind set one toe in the hovel. I couldn't imagine anyone considering for one split second living in that awful place, and there I was inside with a shady character—back in the jewelry store, trapped. Only my eyes moved: darting, assessing, and watching for his move so that I could make mine, startlingly afraid that I would freeze. It was clear; if I lived through the experience, it was time to find another job.

At karate class I overheard a conversation between two women, one of whom was studying psychology. The subject of psychology resonated with me, yet until that moment, I never entertained the notion of school. Perhaps it was the next path to take to finally make sense of my life. In spite of protests from others who said I was too old to start over, I enrolled in a community college. Because John was faithful in his child support payments I could attend school full-time without working. Oddly, my boss was sad to see me go.

Continuing in my spiritual pursuits, I accepted an invitation to Siddha Yoga, pleasantly surprised to find that it was chanting and meditation. At last I was home. At last I belonged. Jacqueline was comfortable there; she enjoyed the experience and happily fit in to the group. I was no longer an oddity, teased about my non-traditional beliefs, or the butt of jokes about vegetarianism—I was with like-minded people. Quite quickly I was initiated at the ashram in California by the Guru during her timely visit from India: a transcendent experience dazzling beyond description. My connection with the group was grounding, deeply satisfying and long-lasting.

I was drawn to participate in a weekend encounter group I knew little about. With the irritating, tiny voice in my head bent on scaring me off and my stomach doing the rumba, on a Friday evening I walked through that door by myself—a really brave thing for me—committed to complete the weekend. I brought no specific issues in my quest for wholeness. I was there to see what showed up.

A bunch of strangers, we arranged ourselves in a large circle, furtively checking one another out, each of us draped in apprehension for what was to come in our common search for answers. I jerked around to see whose voice whispered in my head, *she's fifteen*. Suddenly, the past was there buck naked, poked awake by a young woman in the group talking about a relationship issue with her mother. *Is my daughter really out there somewhere? Is she safe? Is she even alive?* It seemed a mother would know those things about her child.

It was the first time guilt ever raised its voice. *Wait a minute! I'm the victim. It was their fault, not mine.* Guilt did not flinch and the putrid stench of its ugly armpit stayed. I turned on *myself* for the first time. I did not consider the impact of adoption on *her* life: a life without knowing her roots, her mother, where I was and why I relinquished her. *What have I done? How could I have allowed it to happen?*

The next day we each made a "Shit List." My list was both long and short. Just one word, "adoption," ran in a column down the page. Asked to share out loud one item from our list I wanted to leave, but my body would not let me move. I opened my mouth, no sound came out. I opened it again, nothing. Stillness in the room sucked up all the air and stuffed it in my ears. My mouth spoke on its own terms with its own words—unpredicted moans and shrieks shot out ambushing all of us with unexpected dread. Simultaneously, labor pains pulled my chest to my knees. I doubled over in hysterics, my arms folded clutching my belly, and I rocked back and forth, screaming, "My baby, my baby, I want my baby..."

My body clearly in charge, I was only along for the ride. Men carried me from the hushed audience who, like me, wondered what the heck just happened. I remained on a couch in the next room until the pain and crying stopped and my body handed back the controls. As quickly as I could, I regained composure, assured those tending me I had recovered, when really I hadn't, and rejoined the group trying to sidle unseen into my seat. Expectantly, they looked at me en masse. *Great! They saw me. How embarrassing. How am I supposed to explain? What can I say that makes any sense?* I was just as knocked out by my body's performance as they were. My body actually expressed our loss better than any words I could say—I said nothing.

*

My body led the way—flinging out pain it could no longer stomach. I had no choice but to follow its wisdom. Using journaling, I discovered rotting dead bodies: smelly feelings frantic for freedom, eager to vomit venom for my parents that filled notebook after notebook with acrimonious puke I thought would never end. I scribbled, cursed, stabbed holes in the pages with the point of my pen, scraped furiously over paper terrain, ripped through pages too incensed, too infuriated to write: sometimes senseless scrawled markings of a child; sometimes, one word shrieked large on page after page after page of fury ... and tears, lots of tears. I screamed myself hoarse into pillows and beat the bed with a baseball bat until my shoulders burned.

I felt cheated by all the things my father never gave me. Unwittingly, I searched for him in all male relationships itching to find a dad to fill the void he left, to play out with them the relationship I wildly wanted with him.

I never felt loved or worthwhile with my dad, or with men, because a kid with a crayon decided she was insignificant and scribed it onto her heart. *I need someone to love me so that I can love me, so I can be worth something.*

Walking in my mother's footsteps I chose men with barren hearts, emotionally bankrupt men, men that hurt my heart the way it hurt in childhood. She had chosen my dad; a man that never kissed or hugged me, not once.

When an emotionally impoverished, bright-eyed, rebellious jock named Jeff showed up, of course, we attracted like metal to a magnet. My starving heart sold me on being the one to change him. Jeff cheated on me like my dad cheated on my mother: not with physical relationships, emotional ones. He coveted females on television and in movies. Out together in public, his eyes and attention danced over other women, not over me. He said I was ugly when I smiled, that I should firm up my body, and what was wrong with me that I didn't.

Non-physical abuse is the most treacherous: deeply damaging, a massive internal bruising, and a secret bleeding to death of life. His behavior was all too familiar. I thought it was love because it hurt. I thought love was supposed to hurt.

My father's dispassion towards my mother was my frame of reference for relationships. I concluded that women were safe as long as they made no demands and allowed men to do as they wished. If not, they got smacked down or abandoned. The flipside of pleasing made it my fault or failure when someone else was unhappy, when relationships didn't work, when anything went awry. Deceptively adult-like on the outside, inside a frightened little girl with distorted values, all dressed up in wobbly high heels and red lipstick ran my life.

Jeff's mood controlled my feelings; when he accepted me I accepted myself. When his face was indifferent, I automatically tapped into inherent worthlessness cursing myself for it. I stayed with him as my mother stayed with my dad. I stayed because the next day his face could smile and I would be *good enough* again. I stayed because compromising myself was second nature because I didn't know how to leave. Clearly, with his actions he was letting me go. Refusing to be fired, the dope who went back to work at her desk, was the dope that stayed to work on Jeff.

Ticked off about something, I surprised myself by rashly telling Jeff he needed to change his ways. He lashed back. His lack of intimacy became my fault. I gave so much; there was no room for *him* to give. When he went jogging, Brownie, his dog, madly excited, jumped all around him. When he made plans with me I acted like Brownie. I cleaned his house, did his laundry when he left clothing at my apartment, and fixed dinner for him. I tried to be the mother he never had. He was right. I did those things. *I was taking care of him. If that's the wrong way, what's the right way?*

Pleasing doesn't work. It's supposed to! He hated it. He left me. Jeff and I were emotional wrecks. It wasn't my job to rescue him or sacrifice myself trying, erroneously I thought it was. When he wanted me back, I never turned around.

My father was openly quiet, secretly wild. *If I let go would I be wild too? Do quiet people unpredictably explode in frightening violence? Would I?* The product of volatile, raging parents, genetically prepped to be just like them, would I whip people verbally like my mother or physically like my father? Could I trust the part of myself that spewed rank, written anger to confine it to paper—or would it erupt and flip me into the lurking, unpredictable, inherited side, snatched forever from my safe nest of niceness?

*

The more I wrote, the more the coffin of grief for my baby surfaced. Afraid to open it, sheer desperation dragged me into counseling with Mary, who popped up seemingly from nowhere at that most vulnerable time. Supposed to hold my hand as I opened that burial chamber, Mary wanted to begin with the family-of-origin issues I wanted to ignore. *I am at my wits end with those issues. I don't want to do this now!* Of course, she expected me to do the most difficult thing of all: talk, which is why the average person goes to counseling in the first place. However, I was not your average person. Besides, I just wanted support for the next round, the one that really mattered—my missing baby.

Mary went fishing; of all things, she hooked David. Settling in next to me on the couch was too invasive, instinctively my body pulled back into its shell: locked up and unavailable, my mind already elsewhere. She handed me a step-by-step, written exercise, expecting me to verbally walk through the incident with David, right there, with her. *Is she mad? I can't go back there by myself, never mind with a stranger. If she thinks I'm hooking up with those derelict emotions, she's gravely mistaken.* The notion alone of reliving the assault terrified me. Besides, intimately exposing my degradation to her, or anyone, was unthinkable. *Can she even fathom just how much borrowed, beyond me, strength it took to get me to her office? I want to uncover my baby, not the skeleton memory called David.* I read rote words on a page as if they were a recipe. Mary told me I was the most controlled person she had ever met. Her assessment of me felt like an attack. *Is that right? How does she think I survived?*

After opening the wound, Mary left me no choice. Confronting David in my journal, I blurted out anger in thousands of words over countless tear-stained pages. David thought I didn't matter. He thought no one would know if he took license with me. He thought no one would care and so, he gave himself permission to be predatory. He was right, no one knew. He was wrong about the caring. My mother cared; she would have lambasted him. Not knowing exactly what David did to me made me crazy, until I made not knowing okay. Supposed to be my protectors, instead my dad and big brother were the enemies.

Finally, Mary was helpful with the loss of adoption. She suggested that naming my baby and journaling to her would further the healing process. The name, irrelevant now, helped make my baby real rather than imaginary.

Chapter Ten

Awakening Awareness

MY PAST WOULD not shut up. Writing brought everything whirling overwhelmingly to the surface, exacerbating my desire to voice it, to let it go. This is what drew me to the anonymity of an Adult Children of Alcoholics (ACA) meeting. Guarded against expressing anything which could portray me as inferior or inadequate (in my eyes, just about everything), I continued, for acceptance, to fake perfection in the eyes of the world around me. In reality, I scantily survived the internal hell of living up to my self-imposed expectation of being needless like my mother. *Will I be held hostage listening to others—my own life on mute?* Listening kept the attention off me but I had had enough! If ACA was not the safe place I imagined it to be, and I had no assurance it was, with a gut full of dynamite, sooner or later I would spontaneously combust.

In a small group, bit-by-bit I voiced rational pieces of my past—not maniacally as in my journal—actively alert for disapproval, which, astonishingly, never came. In weekly groups I talked without interruption, correction, advice, or disapproval. When gutsy others shared their trials, I was touched by their humanness, their authenticity, and their vulnerability. When they shared victories over their past, promise breathed into my personal hell-hole. Secure in the safety net they created, and bolstered by their courage, I began opening the tomb.

Patrick was a regular at ACA meetings. Hippie-like, not in a derogatory sense, a distinctive one: long hair, sporting a beard, decked out in charisma, his alluring blue eyes, which quite frankly required a permit to own and operate, magnetically drew my gaze. Tall, boyishly slender, long legs snug in blue jeans; well-developed in the art of social chitchat; articulate and interesting; he spoke with authority, and at length. Perfect. He could talk and I wouldn't have to. Predictably hijacked by anxiety in social situations, I hid. But, with Patrick it was different, superficial banter was fun; I forgot to be bothered. We merged on all levels: physical, mental, emotional, and spiritual. Both vegetarians, both piqued by psychology, we both meditated. What a fit. That slice of heaven was a breath of fresh air.

Emotionally speaking, our relationship was a significant improvement over any that came before, and there was intimacy—to a point. I fixed that point. With bedraggled bags of shame and secrets dragging behind me everywhere I went, I had learned to gag myself—to keep my bags fastened—to keep anything unsavory from spilling out to betray me. Patrick brought his own bag of quirks to the mix; there was no dearth of dysfunction in our space.

Stuck in the inescapable crucible of childhood, I felt the same responsibility to care-take Patrick that I felt for my mother. My mind's steady focus trained on Patrick like a pair of binoculars, trying to figure out his needs and wants, trying to be in lock step, detouring disapproval, care-taking in lieu of communication.

Caught in conversations that demanded self-disclosure, electric shocks fried my nerves. Deflecting attention worked sometimes. Sometimes I felt cornered.

He wanted a partner, a lover, not a mother. *Not again! Had I learned nothing from Jeff?* When I told him I would change, I meant it. I wanted to. *I have no idea how to do things differently.* His words said he didn't want someone who did everything for him; yet he let me do it. His token participation was helping prepare nightly meals. When he washed his dinner dishes I resented that he didn't wash mine. Is that what lovers did, clean up only after themselves? If he wanted a snack, he got it without asking if I wanted something too. I felt slighted. Was that selfish or was he simply taking care of himself? If he was, I had a lot to learn. *Am I supposed to care only about me and do nothing for him? Do I leave his dirty laundry: only wash mine? Should I stop housecleaning, changing bed linens and bath towels and wait for him to do it?*

With questions and no answers, I stayed the same, acting, as he said, like a roommate. Perhaps lovers could speak up, ask for what they want, expose their past and express their true feelings. If not, are they just roommates?

He wanted what was hardest in the world for me to do—be vulnerable. *I can't trust anyone with my secrets. I don't want to give them ammunition to shoot me down, no way.* Why couldn't he have just wanted something simple like clean laundry? He asked for the moon and I could barely reach the fence.

If I had known how to stop the nicety of catering to others, I might have done that. *Nice* was grooved into me like fingerprints. *Nice* saved me from confrontations with verbally combative people for whom I was no match, and who could swallow me whole without a drink of water. It saved me from being hurt badly, which petrified me. I reasoned that if my mother had been nice to my dad all the time, he would not have hurt her. The terror I felt when he hit her was alive and thriving in the frightened child squelched down inside but who emerged more and more to the surface. Wanting to be safe, I bought the belief that subservience and submission assured safety. It was a comfort zone I was ill-equipped to leave.

I came into this life fragile, delicate as blown glass. I put myself on an unstable shelf called "chaotic childhood." I put myself in the predicament of finding stability in an always unbalanced place, forever finding ways to not fall off and crash.

They were primitive ways and fear was a big one; it kept me stuck, unmoving, unspeaking lest I fell. That is how I survived it all. It was fear. Fear befriended me in childhood: held my hand when no one would and nothing else could; it led me when I could only follow; and let my mind take me away from things unbearable. But childhood ways were not functional ways, and fear was no more than an addiction, an irreverent keeper from whose seduction and fake security I needed to unfasten myself like a hooker from her pimp. *How is* that *possible? How do I unhook from fear's grasp?*

*

In order to move forward I had to go back; face my past to be free. When I began opening unsettling doors to the tomb, ancient anesthesia that numbed brutal pain, vaporized. Rabid, raw feelings no longer locked down, jumped on me like muggers in a dark alley. I battled against Patrick from the outside; against myself from the inside; simultaneously grieving a colossal loss. The stress of it all wore my nerves wafer thin.

My journaling became markedly more emotional and tormented; I couldn't find words to express the pain. I sat on the floor, back against the couch for support, tears streaming. The air broody, foreboding—unmistakably, death was in the room. I couldn't move. I was the commandeered vessel for that unsettling scene.

By itself, my jaw dropped slightly open. From a vortex that used to be my mouth, out streamed ominous, haunted banshee wailing, crying, moaning—a lingering, piteous funeral procession of sorts, arms linked, holding on to one another for succor in endless mourning. Sounds not unlike wolves howling pierced into night's void—sounds which make all that hear them shiver.

I reverenced this electrifying experience I was privy to: witnessing pain at its most base, most primitive. It actually felt spiritual. Much later I understood its significance. It was my primal scream; a wound in the soul of a broken heart, a weeping inside for my lost child, releasing pain I struggled to express with words that do not exist.

The predicament of, *she was born, but I never gave birth*, stubbornly messed with my emotions. Intermittently, intellectually I knew she was no longer in my belly *but I never felt her leave it. I never saw a baby. I never saw her.* My right to participate in the birth of my child somehow forfeited, I failed to stop the doctor from furtively taking her from my body; taking her away from me; denying my eyes from seeing her; denying me a chance to choose differently. Then it struck me, it was time to let that go to find forgiveness and lay blame to rest.

When I learned people are as sick as their secrets and that family secrets tend as if by osmosis to be repeated, I knew I had to tell Jacqueline about my baby. A year had passed with Patrick.

I planned to tell him first for feedback, for confirmation that I was right to tell my daughter.

Of course I cried. It was the first time the lining of my gut spoke. My own ears winced as bitterness babbled out and curdled the air. *The accursed twenty-three year old, she did it. A good Catholic girl, I could never engage in such sleaze. She sinned and framed me, leaving my belly pregnant, leaving me vilified. Did she know how she tarnished me? How she left me by myself in the sewage of shame? How could she? She deserves to pay for it all. If I have my way she will never cease paying. I despise her.*

Patrick's face neither fell off in disgust, nor did he flee from me in horror. Calmly, he pointed out truth I didn't want to hear. *She was me... is me*: a separated part, some trick of my mind, some effect of trauma, something set up so that I could live through the unlivable.

The vicious scorn I spat at her was hatred for me. *I don't want to be her. I don't want to be responsible for the sex, the pregnancy and the adoption. It's not fair. She's bad. I'm good.* I would rather have blamed her than take responsibility. Finally, some self-disclosure he could get his teeth into, partially pacified this man with a strong need to support. While he needed to feel needed, I needed to be in control. I did not want the errant twenty-three year old mussing what mattered most—my *good girl* persona.

Eventually, with Patrick's acceptance, then my own, resistance softened and I decided to let her in. Quietly, in meditation, holding the intention of forgiveness, I sensed her timidly slip out from the shadows: an unwashed, waif-like creature, eyes cried pale. She peeped warily through straggly strands of hair. My heart couldn't help itself, it melted. As I reached out to hold her, an angel glistening in gossamer swept us into a twirling ecstasy of brilliant light, compassion, and love. Calling the twenty-three year old my *inner child* made our reconciliation more intimate, more appealing.

With compassion from the angel still fresh, I nourished our relationship as if it were a flesh-and-blood one: journaling my voice, sometimes hers, comforting the child she truly was, even at twenty-three. At a time when I couldn't find permission to love myself, a way was graciously given: for in comforting my inner child, I comforted me. Disassociating from emotions that would have caved us both into madness, and saving up pain that took two of us to shoulder kept us sane and alive. I assured her it was the best she could have done at the time, and I assured myself the same. I was ready to confess.

Chapter Eleven

Moving Through the Morass

WE SAT AT THE dining room table. I wanted something solid in front of me; something to grab on to; something tangible to ground me in reality. I needed to keep in check my cheeky emotions, feral children that they were: they could run unpredictably amuck at my body's bidding and frighten her. I told Jacqueline I had a secret to tell, and I cried. She cried because I did. Fear drained her face; her fourteen year old mind actively second guessing. Revealing a faded past that seemed to belong to someone else, to her of all people—she who esteemed me the most—was humiliating. She dared not breathe as I spoke, dropping her shoulders and her face with relief when the secret was out and less dire than the worst she imagined I might say.

Voicing the past to Patrick and Jacqueline began the process of bringing my child to life in *my* life. Jacqueline always wished for a sister. She wanted me to search right then and there. *I need to breathe. It's too soon. I don't even know if she's real. I talk about her as if she were. What if she isn't? Maybe I had some kind of breakdown in the past. Is she really real?* Disclosing was a leap across the Grand Canyon without a net. I made it, and even my body behaved. A mother's love gave me the guts to jump. Who knew where it would take me next.

Jacqueline worked as a grocery clerk after school. When a customer told her she was the image of a friend who was adopted, Jacqueline flew after the customer into the parking lot to enquire more about the friend. Yes, the friend was adopted, but further details made it clear it was not her sister. She scrutinized faces for those who resembled herself, wondering if she would recognize her own sister.

Jacqueline and Patrick, tongues hanging out to get started, couldn't understand why I dragged my feet to search. Used to processing things by myself in my head, it never occurred to me to let them in on how I juggled the pros and cons of searching. My heart, however, was crystal clear… *How can a mother* not *search?* That was always my secret stance.

Spiteful, the small voice in my head ran its ugly mouth beating me up like a gang banger earning his initiation right. *How could the God of my childhood be that heartless? Where was my credit for past good behavior as a Catholic school girl? Where were the ministering angels that are supposed to exist? Why didn't He send me one person, just one single person, one lousy person to help me then? Was that too much to ask? I want my baby back. I want her.* I stabbed holes in my journal with a furious pen and beat cushions to death with a berserk baseball bat.

I went back to clobbering my dad. Venting everything distasteful in drunkenness that he passively packed away in quietness; saving it up, he spewed focused madness on his mate, indiscriminately splattering his offspring, stamping trauma on impressionable, terrified young minds. Booze unleashed his verbal vomit. I was stuck with quiet, without a release. Quiet helped me cope as a child, but I was no longer a child. I was an adult with the mindset of a child. Wanting to ditch quiet because quiet was a dead-end street, how was I supposed to express myself without losing control, without annihilating the other person? Afraid to get angry out loud, I voiced anger only on paper and when hiking. *What am I supposed to do?* My adult knew I had to do things differently—but how?

Sober, my father slammed doors and left, chased out by conflict. I too have retreated from conflict in the same way. Picturing my dad in a more compassionate light, I saw a frightened little boy framed as an adult, overwhelmed with a litter of kids, clueless how to be a committed, loving father and husband. His fear and avoidance of responsibility came through liquor and cheating. He had to look perfect, dressed up, grown up. Perhaps escaping into new clothing, clothed in a symbolic way some unfathomable wound within him.

I cared on the inside, but damned if it came out. I wonder if he cared on the inside. My heart has chosen to believe he did. He was trapped like me, in the mortuary of silence. The anger I witnessed, and felt the brunt of as a child, convinced me that anger itself was bad. Consequently, I handled that perceived deadly emotion gingerly: like a hand grenade whose pin could carelessly fall out causing external maiming and mayhem; oblivious to the destruction it wrought unexpressed, inside me. I never told my dad I loved him—does that mean I didn't? My dad never said he didn't love me. Erroneously, I wrote *I am unloved, thus unlovable* into the secret script of a child's mind and played it out in real life.

Chapter Twelve

Unstoppable

IT WAS TIME to search. Jacqueline was thrilled. *What would it be like to actually find her? Would she want us? Would she even like us?* Finding her mattered, we would deal with the rest. My heart beat like an African drum—surprisingly no one turned to see the source of such a racket in the library. I surrounded the completed paperwork to Search Triad and to Soundex Reunion Registry (SRR) with white light and a prayer to God to guide its journey, returning results for the highest and best good of us all. It then slipped silently, unceremoniously from my hand into the mailbox for delivery.

It seemed there should have been some kind of pageantry for such a momentous event, perhaps a marching band. Important not to drop search-initiating papers into the convenient mailbox near my home, the receptacle in front of the library had more appeal as a dignified, proper send off. Making my first move in that public place, symbolized my standing up openly to an era that once held me captive. Forging ahead to find her, liberated me from the need for society's approval. More than a comforting gesture, it was empowering.

If she was registered with SRR, our match would be instant. She was not registered—*she is not looking for me*—there was no match. Search Triad aids adoptees and birth families in their searches. The night of my initial Search Triad meeting I wanted to be cool, in control, convince others I had my act together with my emotional baggage unpacked, aired and ironed.

For the prior two weeks that felt true—pain's tentacles retracted back to their habitual hideout. Perhaps they were gone for good. *Please be over. I can't take much more of it.*

I was curious about the other women I'd meet: *What kind of women are they? What do they look like? What should I expect?*

At six o'clock it hit me; I was going to *that* meeting. Long in coming, finally there, its arrival shook me up. I cried. I was afraid to go, and by myself. *Why do I have to do the hardest things in my life alone?* I wanted to escape, but the desire to go was stronger. To find her, I had to do what I feared most: open up to others.

Secretly envisioning birth mothers as streetwalkers, immoral prostitute types, I self-righteously assumed myself their superior, outclassing them, conspicuous in the grave differences between us—projecting that sullied image onto them because I felt sullied. To pretend my issues were resolved was nonsense. *I need to find her to heal.*

Startlingly, those brave women were just like me—ordinary, decent, with usual everyday lives, homemakers to heads of businesses, mothers joined by the commonality of loss, missing something so precious, so profound—they too sought reunion. With uncommon courage and eyes on the goal, unstoppable, they wholeheartedly stepped into the unknown to search, unfolding themselves and their lives to complete the past and build something new in the present. Their stories, journeys successful thus far, and not so, were touching. As a group, the women took care of their physical selves, perhaps wanting to look their best when their children were reborn into their lives.

For some months prior to initiating the search, following meditation, I brought my baby into awareness, envisioning how it would feel to hold and love her. No doubt this nudged me into action. Perhaps it was my inner child's mind that always fastened on the baby, never the adult. Part of me was so excited that I had launched my search; I wanted to scream it to the world. The other part wanted to hide under the bed. Bolstering myself with positive self-talk, I built myself up for the reunion much like athletes build themselves physically for a major event. I wanted that kind of strength for whatever came next.

*

Search Triad linked me with a birth mother who successfully completed her own search; she became my mentor. I would have preferred almost anything to picking up the phone. I picked it up anyway, called the hospital, and requested my birth records. Unprepared for a snippy female's couldn't-care-less attitude, "You gave your baby up for adoption, you're not entitled to those records," I hung up in tears. First step a failure, I was furious. How dare she flick me away like an irritating bug?

Loss flooded in; I was back in the past fondling thoughts of the newborn I never held. The soft fingers that never held mine, her first word, first step, first tooth. Instead, I felt those experiences had been taken from me and I was outraged.

It was not the adoptive mother I railed against, it was the rules. As I understand it, women that cannot bear their own children suffer similarly to birth mothers. Perhaps, they even feel cheated out of the gift of childbirth by Nature, as I felt cheated by the doctor, out of the experience of childbirth. I imagine some have their own secretive primal screams, their own inexpressible internal loss, and with desires so desperate to have a child, they adopt another's.

The desperation those women have for a child is the same desperation I had to keep my child, the same desperation to find her. Adoption is a failure of sorts for us both; I can't keep my child, and she can't conceive her own child. Adoption is a loss for us both: loss of my child to adoption and the loss of her child to infertility. Birth and adoptive mothers are more alike than different. Compassion is due both. With Patrick's encouragement, I called the hospital back. A kind woman told me I *was* entitled to records including those of my labor and delivery.

Following the Search Triad meeting, I was lost in thoughts of my child. Intrusive pain that two weeks earlier seemed resolved walked in without knocking; it never really went away. It only slept. The grieving never ended but lay in waiting like a cobra to catch me at unsuspecting moments. *It has no resolution. No one told me the pain was permanent. No one told me not to do it, or said it was a mistake, or that the pain would last forever.* How *could* the grieving end?

There was no death with which to finally come to terms; it is a living, ongoing death as she's alive, somewhere. Ideal families, adoptive or otherwise, in reality, do not exist. I can only hope those that had my child prized her. Having Jacqueline gave me the glory and esteem of motherhood, but my irreplaceable child was still missing. Without her, I was incomplete. As a mother interrupted, my grief never magically ceased. It stayed—the missing stayed.

Woven into every fiber of my being, how could anyone tell me, a mother, to forget my child? Society's disapproval had the power to mandate a mother's mind into pretending she never had a child, effectively condemning her to unfathomable depths of unimaginable, depraved, cruel, isolated pain. But a mother's heart can never be ordered to forget her loss. Asking the moon to throw a blanket over her glow, to no longer light up the night sky—that has more possibility than asking a mother's heart to forget her baby. With indisputable moral rights to seek out my child, my flesh and blood, I would find her. Surely, then the pain would stop!

I was scared to find her and scared not to. *Who am I to her? What do I say to a grown-up daughter I meet for the first time? Does she look like me, Jacqueline, my family? I wonder if she waited on me in a store or a restaurant and I never recognized her. Perhaps she lives down the street. Perhaps she's a mother herself.* As a daughter, I imagined a greater likelihood of compassion from her, and if she had my emotional make-up, her heart needed barely a nudge to cry. *But she's not looking for me. Is that an omen to leave well enough alone?* I might have honored that sign: quit, lived a safe fantasy of *what ifs.* But I could not. Living with a memorial in my head, my body perpetually mourning in its shadow was not life. Not searching was never a valid option.

An adoptee in the search group nonchalantly asked, "Why did you give up your child in the first place?" *What kind of question is that? Does she really expect me to have a pat answer—a one sentence response? Perhaps my response should be as ridiculous as her question. 'Oh, I was having a bad day!' My child could zing that same question at me! Maybe she's better off not knowing me. What will I say to her? How will I make her understand? Can I cope with backlash from my past from her?* Suddenly, searching did not look so rosy.

I was in the kitchen by the window, feeling the loss of her as if it had just occurred. Insatiable pain sucked dry the juice in my bones, repeatedly coming back to squeeze me for more. That time it made me an offer, which, my brain in a fog, I almost bought: drive into the desert until I am utterly lost, shut my eyes, fling away my car keys, then sit and wait for sweet, predictable relief to come. No turning back. No way out in a moment of forgetting the recurrent chokehold of pain. I turned back too many times only to face familiar torture around the next bend.

Intolerable, screaming walls crashed inside my head. Fighting off demons that would not die—I had no fight left—the dubious trophy of victory was theirs. There was no escape. No matter where I went or what I did pain dogged me, circling like a buzzard salivating eagerly over the coming last gasp of a dying prey. It chased me. Whenever it grabbed me, I wanted to flee, but there was nowhere left to go. My only fathomable way to end suffering was to surrender, cease to exist, have no dwelling left for it to haunt, let the entourage of pain have its revenge.

A tiny spark ignited to save the life I could not un-stick from pain. *I want to end this. You cannot. I can't live with the pain anymore. You can hold on. You can wait. You can make it. What if she comes to find you and finds your grave instead? What kind of mother's love is that? Do you really want that legacy for her?* In my mind's misty jumble I had somehow lost sight of her. Yes, she might find me. She could be at my door tomorrow. I did not want my eyes closed a second time. I could not risk missing her—not again. I would hang on. I would find a way.

My search had pushed me to an edge of sorts. Irrational, I monitored myself the way a mother monitors an impulsive toddler. Impetuously, I wanted to stop women in public I thought were she. In line at the bank, I struggled to keep myself in check: she was the teller, I was sure of it. I wanted to grill her about her life yet I did not, there were people in line behind me. I could unravel reciting my *shit list,* but who would rescue me: pick up the pieces, carry me to sanity if I sat rocking on the floor in the corner of the bank screaming for her? She was *everywhere*. I saw her several times a day as I searched the faces of young women the way I searched previously the faces of babies. I had to restrain myself from approaching them. *Excuse me, are you adopted? I'm searching for my daughter.*

I could not fault my mind for running rampant. It served me well: saved me with denial, saved me from my emotions until I could take them on. It saved my life. My mind was not failing. It was frazzled, fatigued, finished, like the rest of me. Together, we were trying to climb Mount Everest in tennis shoes, and if someone didn't get us off the icy slopes, we wouldn't survive. We needed an outside force to intervene. We, I, needed a miracle.

Chapter Thirteen

You Gotta Get UGLY

MY MOTHER LIVED mostly in turmoil yet she never got lost in life's circumstances. Even when her children died, she somehow kept her stride. She faced responsibilities nose-to-nose, and parented with inherited practices from powerful matriarchs, fixed in her in childhood. When Mam said her grandmother "ruled with a rod of iron," pride and admiration whisked through her eyes as lightening fear grimaced fast on her face.

Disturbingly, it shot straight through me and moved me to compassion for the little girl she once was. *How sad. I wonder how many times she felt the sting of that rod. I see now how she became tagged with toughness.* She thought the world of her own mother, although she never actually said that, still she seemed to revere her grandmother more. Her wise blue eyes held so many secrets about her life that I will never know. *I wonder who held her and kissed her as a child. Did anyone? Who told her that she was precious and beautiful and wondrous? Who told her she was loved? I think no one did, or surely she would have given that to us! She deserved to be snuggled close, showered with kisses and adored with pure abandon. All children deserve that.*

My teachers modeled and sanctioned physical discipline when they used the cane and the leather strap to dole out punishment. This treatment of children raised no eyebrow then. Instead, it gave parents permission to follow suit with their own brand of physical discipline. As a social worker, I encountered parents who, ignorant of other more effective, less punitive ways to parent, disciplined their children as they were disciplined.

They may not have liked the ways in which they were punished by their parents, yet they dutifully passed them on to their own children anyway. After all, as many of them remarked, they themselves turned out okay didn't they!

There was no reason, no incentive for them to look for methods other than those they knew. That was true of my mother. It is obvious to me now, that Mam did the best she could with what she was capable of at the time, without support, with what she knew. Actually, she performed miracles. It is so easy to judge otherwise from the limited perspective of a personal point of view. My mother stood with integrity and resolve in an unvoiced commitment to her children. Did I have such a commitment for my missing child when she was born?

Like me, my mother had no loving father figure, no model of a loving parental relationship. She learned that life was hard; that she needed to be a warrior in many ways to battle her way through it, and she was impeccably that. Outwardly expressing love and affection was not her way: being on guard and invulnerable was. Her work ethic was instilled in her, and at that she excelled. Still, she loved us with a lion's heart. I did not see that then.

Mam had every right to be angry about her life. I took her anger personally. Now I understand that it was not my fault. Her brusque way of being and Spartan tenderness, I also made about me and in my child's mind there was only one conclusion: *She doesn't love me.* Yet not once, ever, did my mother say that she didn't love me—I said it.

She didn't love me the way I thought love was supposed to be. It didn't look the way I thought it should look. Intent on looking at the lie for proof that *she does not love me,* I missed the truth. She loved me with many selfless actions which, as a child, I did not comprehend, but now stare me down. Seeing through her eyes, I recognize that my mother gave us the greatest love of all, her dedicated life. The childhood stories, the made-up lies, thoughts fueled by unverified feelings, steered me towards life characters that proved the fiction to be fact.

I loved my mother conditionally. *Show me you love me. Then I'll love you.* That behavior, of course, came from fear—of her rejection. *What if she didn't love me back? What if she actually spoke those words out loud? I would find somewhere to hide and cry until I died.* Carrying this fear of rejection into my life, I withheld love from just about everyone. As long as no one could get close to me, I felt safe. I held them at bay with an electric prod while I scrutinized, judged, and analyzed them endlessly for proof of their love.

Of course, I never found that proof. I was right: no one could love me. I punished myself: hid myself away; took a back seat in life, all to conceal the inferiority that not even a mother could embrace. And in doing so I wasted a life: I lost a baby and lost myself in lies—*my mother doesn't love me, and neither can you.*

Perhaps like me, Mam faked adulthood, teetered in her high heels, her lipstick also smeared, and belligerence on her tongue to hold the world at bay to shield her own insecurity. Emotionally, a lost five-year-old, an only child, she was now draped with children that religious beliefs encouraged her to produce; she raised a family by herself, constantly manipulating circumstances to survive. Which of her children would be assigned to sneak money from my dad's pocket for milk while he slept? Which co-worker could she borrow money from to tide her over until next payday? How many shillings could she scavenge from the gas meter in order to buy our next meal? Did she ever have a moment's peace? Was there ever a time with no problem to solve?

Money was ubiquitous, an almost inescapable tormentor in our house. My distain for money dissolved when I figured out that it's not money that hurts, it's the lack of it that has painful consequences. If there had been enough money, Mam would not have been crazed when I lost the half crown and I would not have been traumatized. Her rile was not about me, it was about *not* having more money to replace what I lost. My dad didn't break her thumb because she asked him for money, but because to him, there was not enough. Did he have money? Probably, but if he had a poverty consciousness, he was rooted in scarcity thinking. No matter how much or how little he had, he needed the security of it in his breast pocket.

Lack, not money, is the root of all evil. People lie, cheat and steal to avoid it. Perhaps those who resort to these measures are not evil at all. Perhaps, like Mam they are desperate to fill a need, and from where they stand, they see no other avenue.

When I failed to fight David off, I wrote *helpless* on myself in permanent marker; convinced myself that I was a failure; then took on that I was damaged goods. From that point forward, I stationed rescuers throughout my life to do things for me, be responsible for me, and make my choices. I mistakenly smeared blame onto my mother for an inferiority she was blameless in forging. David did not tell me to be helpless either. I created the bars to a self-imposed prison with made-up mantras that crept with venomous legs into every area of my life sucking up my personal power, making me into a victim.

Abused women stay with their abusers for a variety of reasons, economic and emotional: dependency, love, children, religion, fear, approval, secrecy, etc. My mother had those reasons. She was, in a sense, married to Catholicism, a religion which denied her permission to leave.

My mother did not know the impact on me of domestic violence in all its forms. She didn't know I made up *I'm not safe anywhere, ever,* then attached a motion sensor to my mind to scan the constant surroundings for minute flutters of perceived danger. She didn't know I secretly fended off others with *get away; you threaten me,* in a nanosecond of deciding based on hypersensitive, distorted radar. She didn't know that I learned to hide so well that I could be invisible without a magic wand. She just saw me as "shy."

Giving others' actions and words, or lack of them, meanings *I* totally invented, stories *I* concocted, just added more bars to my personal prison. My mother could not fix her child's suffering—she didn't know it was there. To her, I was just quiet. Making up that *quiet is safe,* I bought the duct tape and stifled myself. My own deduced beliefs scalded my soul. Not her.

I translated her fury into *angry people will hurt me . . . don't say a word . . . hide . . . be nice, or else.* She preferred that I stand up for myself. Interpreting my responses to her as talking back, as disrespect, she silenced me. I turned it into a gag order for life. My made-up stories became my own worthless gods of worship.

For the longest time I wrestled to be at peace with my mother. I thought she stole my life. I thought she stole my essence because nothing in me was good—or so I believed: a sad self-summation. Mam and I were emotional strands toggled together: teasing us apart seemed impossible. To forgive her, I had to forgive myself. Not a conscious awareness that needed a conscious fix, it was more of an inner knowing: something to be cognizant of, and to sit with. Bizarre as it sounds, she seemed to be a part of me I wanted to separate from and couldn't: a part I despised.

I was reminded of my twenty-three year old inner child; the initial distain was the same. Then the realization hit: *It was not about my mother at all*—although I foisted blame on her. Shockingly, the distain was about me—flaming anger, easier and safer subconsciously to dress her in than own up to—my 'good girl' façade would never willingly permit that.

Tears, repressed somewhere inside for ages, finally found their escape. Situations flashed through my mind like a slide show as if my inner children, all stages and ages, lined up with their scenarios, revealing themselves to be healed. I was blindsided by abyssal sadness, resonant loss and utter disgust at the degradation of me by me: for all the times I said *yes* and wanted to say *no*; for putting up with so much and keeping my mouth shut; for giving myself away over and over again; for being nice when I didn't want to be; for not taking a stand for myself; for giving in for approval; for letting me be used by others; for shutting up instead of speaking up; for being afraid; for letting others be my voice; for not asking questions; for pretending I understood when I did not; for not telling on David when he attacked me; for pleasing others at my expense; for having sex when I didn't want to; for giving my child away; for abandoning myself, my heart and my soul.

I saw myself, hapless, lost; exposed to the naked truth of it all; trying to cover up *the ugly* with which I had vandalized *myself*. No different than crudely carved initials into the trunk of a tree—I carved *ugly* graffiti on my psyche and into my soul. I felt the scourge of self-inflicted pain. It wasn't my mother that didn't love me—*it was me*. I grieved the irreverent disregard for myself, unbelieving I could be so frivolous, so wasteful with a life, my life.

Yes, I wanted to verbally berate myself and I began to, yet stopped abruptly; somehow, I just knew that it was time to let self-judgment go. I put down my club and embraced it all. Self-compassion and self-forgiveness sweetly and swiftly drifted in, denying my conscious mind any opportunity to reject them. I let them amble about and through me. I let me love me. A chant spontaneously sprang up in my head, "I am enough," and I believed that wholeheartedly.

Something huge had shifted. My armor fell off. Spring awakened in my entire body—birds sang, butterflies fluttered, trees' graceful tendrils swayed in the delicate breeze, and joy danced. For the first time I loved my mother from my heart, not my head. I instinctively knew that I could love her *and* be safe at the same time. And I could love myself. The moment was monumental.

When I saw the devastation of the ugly ways of thinking and the ugly ways of being in my life: how it used me up and threw me like a crumpled-up piece of trash into the garbage, I saw also the antidote, the answer.

In order to transform ugliness, to let go of *the ugly*, you've gotta *get* UGLY (U Gotta Love You). Self-love is not self-ish. Self-love is crucial, a requisite. If I cannot love me, I cannot love you. If I cannot love me, I will crave love from you, and no matter the variety of ways you stand on your head to prove your love, it will never be enough. You cannot fill up what is missing in me. I first have to own it, and then I can accept it.

Taking on UGLY (U Gotta Love You), I let go of who I thought I was. All things happen in their own time. This is love's time. It feels like a truth: that when I honestly love and value me, no one and no-thing can knock me off my center because I own my own love; it is independent of another, none can take it from me. I never again have to grovel for it and the more I give it away, the more it is replenished.

Obviously, the purpose of my meandering life path thus far was about love, about learning to love me, about finding love I thought I never had, could never get, and never even deserved. Spirit gave me back to me. I was humbled, in awe of the Majesty that orchestrated such a marvelous awakening. And I was present to gratitude for every single bit of my life before it, for it brought me to this place. I thought I was searching for my lost child; unknowingly I searched for us both. I was just as lost as she. I was given an opportunity to live newly: to choose differently. I never dreamed that getting UGLY (U Gotta Love You) could be so beautiful. I say, put your heart first and let it lead the way, because first and foremost you gotta *get UGLY (U Gotta Love You)* and get on with life, a life that's worth living. Let go of *the ugly* and *get UGLY*.

All that being said, if we truly do choose our parents and childhood as the fertile soil for the roots of life lessons personally and purposefully picked, as I've read and been told, then there truly is no-thing to forgive. There is simply gratitude for my family for playing their parts so well, and for being the springboard for my life. Childhood does not come to stay…it comes to pass. It wasn't designed to be permanently attached.

My mother may have been wobbling in her high heels while she raised us, yet, with fiery, made-up strength she forged the way and we all came out alive. Sometimes that has to be enough, and that *alone* is worthy of gratitude.

Chapter Fourteen

I'm in Love

Iᴛ ᴡᴀs Cʜʀɪsᴛᴍᴀs Eᴠᴇ. Routinely I opened the mailbox, eyeballed the envelope as if it were an apparition, ripped it open, raced over the page and rushed inside to excitedly blurt out my news. "Danielle. Her name is Danielle." *She is alive. She* does *exist.* Already afternoon, with time enough to squeeze in a few hours of searching and now with new leads to follow, I jumped into my car and sped downtown. She was so close, yet so far away. Although it was almost closing time at the library, I quickly found more clues. Nerves all of a dither in anticipation, I bolted home, hastily flew through the telephone book and, miracle of miracles, there she was in black and white, and in Arizona.

In a mania of emotions, I called my search mentor. We processed my taking time to gather more information before I contacted Danielle. Not to rush to make contact made seeming sense. If I could just see a picture of her, that would be enough. Old school yearbooks were an option. I knew her address. I could stake out her house, catch a glimpse of her and be content.

My mind jostled ideas around until evening, when the impact finally hit. I could not waste another instant. *She's a hair's breadth away.* I wanted to rush headlong into it, contact her there and then; too many years had already passed. *I have waited so long. I have to see her in person.* Nothing less would do.

Trembling, desperately nervous, scared to my wit's end of rejection, and of acceptance, I picked up the phone and dialed, only to hear a male voice on an answering machine. More calls, same thing. It was getting late. I tried one last time.

"Hello," sang a sweet feminine voice. My child's first cry—at last! She sounded like an angel singing. Ribbons of feelings fluttered through my skin. Awestruck, I could not speak. "Hello," she repeated. Thankfully, the recommended words to say were written on a page in front of me, a prompt sheet in the event I was immobilized by any number of feelings. Hoping my voice would speak, stay calm; matter-of-fact, I told her I believed she could help me and asked her to write down my number. Squeezing my left hand tightly so that I wouldn't choke up, I told her my maiden name, named the hospital of her birth, recited the birth date, said I was looking for a young woman born at that place and time and I thought she was that woman. *Click!*

Jacqueline and Patrick sat like statues while I called. Rejection was always a possibility, yet I was shaken and they were floored. I either called her back minutes later or her husband called me; I don't remember which. Whatever he said, I never heard—he was not the one I wanted—I wanted Danielle.

Immediately after, her adoptive father called. The way to my daughter was through him; that irked me. He wanted to check me out—he wanted to meet. My ego was furious. I wanted her, not him. I did not agree to meet, got off the phone as quickly as possible to get myself together and with Jacqueline and Patrick's input, figure out what was next.

Perhaps she wanted to call the shots, be in control, and she had that right. *Perhaps she disowned me long ago and has no desire to retrace the past. Why should she? She doesn't owe me a thing. I could just show up on her doorstep. I don't need him as an intermediary.* I was not willing to let anyone stand in my way, not again. But she was obviously cautious; she hung up on me. *Maybe she asked him to check me out.* I wanted to respect her wishes, her privacy. If she wanted it to play out that way, I would do it...for her.

The search gave me time to prepare myself to find her. She didn't have the advantage of preparation. Perhaps it was best to back off, let her absorb the shock and wait for her to contact me. But I didn't want to wait and I didn't want to play games. Putting ego aside, I called her adoptive father back. We set a time and place to meet and agreed to bring photographs.

Rusty was non-threatening, relaxed, easy to chat with. Tense, past feelings of a young, undeserving unwed mother unshakably present, we swapped photographs and I got my first glimpse of Danielle. Regardless of whose face at first glance she wore, without question she was my longed-for, long lost, finally found daughter!

Rusty asked for details about her birth father, which for two reasons I withheld. No doubt Danielle asked him to bring back that information, but I needed a lure for contact and I wanted to tell her about Lloyd face-to-face. She deserved that. Rusty told stories of Danielle that never made it to a brain intent on wondering when I would see her in person. The photographs were a tease. I wanted the flesh-and-blood woman and I would have to wait. We parted as graciously as we met.

Not ready to meet for what seemed like forever, we wrote back and forth; eventually, prompted by her grandmother, she took a chance. Arriving early at the restaurant, I mindlessly drank coffee; anxiety busily bit my nails. She walked in. I approached her. Like strangers we mechanically hugged, then made our way to the table. Unlike tearful reunions I have since seen on television shows, we neither demonstrated nor expressed strong emotions. I knew she was reticent to be there. I knew she was mine, yet I knew she was not. *This is confusing. What is my role here?*

Cautiously controlled, captured in wonderment, perhaps I had slipped to the fantasy side of my mind and she was real in my imagination only. She owned Lloyd's dark hair, my emerald eyes, his spectacular black lashes and enticing, charmed smile. Outstandingly beautiful, drawn to her spellbound, fairies danced around us sprinkling magical dust. The longer she filled my gaze the more entranced I became, falling hopelessly in love with her alluring beauty.

A familiar connection ran through my senses as my soul beaming, caressed hers. *She is mine. She came from me. How can she not be irresistible to me?* I could not, but my heart leapt out kissing her all over. I wanted to. I wanted to hold her. I wanted to touch her, caress her, but I could not. That was not appropriate, there were boundaries. As I gazed, I wondered where the baby was, trying to imagine how my baby could be in that adult body. I sat, at last, miraculously next to my long-lost daughter, but I wanted the baby too.

Her life was good, with wonderful adoptive parents and a younger adopted sister. She was involved in all the activities a child could want: she had a large, extended, close adoptive family, and was deprived of nothing. She seemed stiff, defensive, protective, as if loyalties to her adoptive family were threatened and I somehow put all that was her life at risk.

She said she knew she had been adopted, even before she understood the concept of adoption. Bearing no resemblance to her adoptive family, sometimes when she looked in the mirror she wondered who it was she resembled. She wanted to know about and meet her birth father. I agreed to search.

Relating the marvel of Danielle to Jacqueline and Patrick, I luxuriated in the bliss of being in love. But *all* was not bliss. *I want my baby. Where is my baby? Where can I look?* Trying to fantasize the baby filled out into the adult was fruitless. *I want my baby.* My mind simply could not comprehend she no longer existed. Actually, it was not simple at all. It was difficult, very, very difficult. None in my search group that reunified told me how to find the baby. None said she would still be missing. None told me what to do, how to handle the yearning. I found the woman that was my baby, but my baby was still missing. *How am I supposed to resolve this?*

Chapter Fifteen

Completing the Past

UNANNOUNCED, I SHOWED up at Lloyd's door. Danielle and I drove separately. Danielle waited in her car while I stood brazen, knocking at an unfamiliar potential portal to what seemed like a previous life. The door was whisked scarily open by a familiar-faced ghost wearing well his youthful charm. *I'm doing it for Danielle* I reminded myself; doubtful I could have done it for any other reason.

With a handful of words, I reminded him who I was; he invited me inside. When I mentioned Char's name a smile licked his face, my stomach turned. Maturity was wasted on him. His boyish impropriety was blatant. The conversation was clipped, brief. He sat. I stood. The unfitting photograph of a blonde-haired girl grabbed my attention. His look was changeless as I disclosed the adoption and search. I made no confrontations; he made no refutes. He didn't need to. He knew he was safe from legal reprisals, if there ever were any.

He did not relocate to California as he had said and was in Arizona all along. *What?* I wanted to flee to gulp in air. Lacking the wherewithal to consider saving face, he made no attempt at vindication. Years evaporated and there I was eye-to-eye with the male who deserted me: staked me on an anthill in the desert; left me for dead; left me for buzzards that came with certainty. *I have to stay focused for her sake.* His complacency awed me. *I want to make him feel something.*

Everything in me had eyes on the door. *I'm doing this for her* made me stay. Danielle wanted his picture. Unaware that searching was a possibility, that I would ever actually set eyes on her, I ripped his picture to bits years before. He jumped up, seemed eager to pacify, perhaps only to get rid of me, and found a small younger picture of him and handed it over.

He pointed to the photograph of the blonde girl who looked nothing like him: his daughter. He wanted to protect her from knowledge of Danielle; her trust in him was delicate and he didn't want to chance it. At Danielle's request I gave him my phone number not hers. He agreed to make arrangements through me, to meet her.

Lloyd contacted me a couple of times to finalize arrangements with Danielle. Both times he was irritated, abrasive for no apparent reason. The restaurant temperature and server where they met displeased Lloyd, so they left and dined elsewhere. He was pleasant to Danielle, told her she bore the strongest resemblance to him of all his children, including an almost look-alike son that lived overseas. He also mentioned the daughter he was protecting.

Married a handful of times; currently single; a recovering drug and alcohol addict, Lloyd had spent serious, accumulated time in sobriety. He answered Danielle's questions about her heritage and promised her photographs.

Meeting him later, quite by chance at a coffee house, I was inexplicably mesmerized. He worked me with his smile, eyed me up and down and, I have to admit, his baiting charm had not lost its allure. There he stood, blatantly alive, smiling, dressed in the good life, happy, acting as if nothing life-changing had happened and we were long-lost acquaintances catching up on the trivia of our lives. Yet, his conversation was all about him. Captured in shock, I navigated small talk like a nervous, twittering bird. Before our encounter ended, I mentioned the pictures he promised Danielle, as he had seemed sincere in his commitment to follow through. He was moving out of state he said—*hmm, how familiar.*

I did not vomit rage over Lloyd in our chance meeting because I was hogtied by his charm; by my own insecurity; and because I knew that, while he did walk away from me, he did *not* make me give up Danielle, although lingering resentment wanted so badly to bash him. I had bashed him senseless in my journal too many times to count; screamed out fury in my car while driving and into pillows at home; and punched it out in karate. He did not say he was leaving, then, *"Oh, by the way, adopt the baby out."* That was *my* doing. He simply said he was leaving.

I know nearly nothing of his past, but it seemed he had his own inner demons that took their toll. He apparently lost a chunk of his life to drugs and alcohol. I lost a chunk of mine to blame, an addiction of sorts. It was *way* past time for inner peace. Lloyd did not follow through with the promised photographs. We neither saw nor heard from him again. Danielle's purse with his small picture inside was eventually lost.

My baby was still missing. Quieting my mind, I sat with my inner child, calming her primal scream, soothing us both with compassion, seeking the acceptance that would bring us both peace.

*

In meditation, I embraced everyone even remotely connected to the adoption, but forgiveness was not instant. It took time to stick.

A seeker of answers, I continued to participate in various life-exploring venues that seemed to choose me; wondering how on earth I ended up there, always ultimately glad that I did. They fast forwarded my journey.

Twenty minutes into a course preamble, tears crept out. Suddenly, David was there. I didn't bring him. I didn't want him. I tried to ignore my emotions and shove him from my brain, but he wouldn't go. In spite of my reluctance to even think about him, it was time, ready or not, to release David. *I don't want to do this—not in front of other people! Why do I have to do this now? Why not at home, by myself, in the security of my own living room?*

The entire room partnered up, mine ended up being the ideal dyad. Hopefully, I would not be a spectacle. Thankfully, the room quickly became a sea of avid voices. Several times my mouth opened to speak and closed again—only air came out. I shifted about in my seat. My body began to shake; sobs followed;

then stuttered, chopped-up words mixed with air. I made it through David's attack; and I didn't die!

For the first time, out loud and present, I relived the past to put it behind me. In time, I grasped that sexual assault really is about control and power. I truly believe David's attack was not personal, but that he *is* responsible for his actions. His behavior was spawned by the environment in which we were raised, and for that I found compassion. David loved me and I loved David. In my heart, I know his purpose was not to harm me. I never spoke about the incident with David, now deceased. Finally I forgave my brother, and myself. When I forgave him, I loved him even more.

In a later seminar, as he stood on the podium stairs, a male participant unexpectedly erupted in a feigned display of frighteningly real anger, bringing my past palpably present. My dad was standing at the top of the stairs. He was wearing his long-sleeved shirt; his fist was raised, ready to strike my mother. Without warning my body began to shake uncontrollably. I managed to get to my feet, although I couldn't walk or speak. A palaver ensued and someone called 911. In the past, I had fainted in church: the familiar feeling breezed over me as the room dimmed. The man next to me scooped me up, carried me out of the room and stood me on my feet. Gesturing that I wanted to get outside, he supported me as I wobbled there. I had to get out of the building. I had to escape.

Years since my body's last colorful performance, that was its finest. The intensity of its reaction and of my panic disturbed me. *I can't trust my body. Will it suddenly take over when I'm driving? What if I'm at work; I'll never be able to explain it.* My whole body ached for about a week; before long, distrust faded.

That grand scale expression tossed things around inside and created space for something else to emerge. What emerged in a follow-up course was startling. I went with the intention of completing the past with my dad, as I had always accused him of withholding love from me. What I discovered was that *I* withheld love from *him*, to punish him for hurting my mother. The moment that awareness tapped my heart, judgment of my dad disappeared and delectable waves of love washed eagerly in to take its place. Head over heels in love with my dad is delicious bliss. At last I know how a dad's love feels—it's better than raspberry ripple ice cream.

When I called John to absolve him of blame for the adoption of Danielle, he cried and put down his cross. In layers, gradually I gave up bitterness and blame of everyone else for the loss of my child. Then I took responsibility for all of it—including the pregnancy—that way I held life's reigns. I, alone, made the choices. Taking responsibility is empowering. The alternative, well, that's the path of victimhood.

Finally, I recognized the ministering angels along my path, and John was one of them. He cared for me, loved and protected me, and my baby was part of me. Had he disowned and discarded me, in my muddled state of mind, what would we have done? He not only went out on a limb for us, he sheltered us. Without John's protective wings about us, who knows how, or if, my baby and I would have made it. John never told me to give Danielle up for adoption, although the loaded rifle of blame held him in its long-range sights. Adoption was *my* choice.

For the longest time God, to me, was a bounty hunter stalking me for His reward—and my punishment. A God fashioned from the human traits of paybacks and penalties, I divorced myself from Him; found my own face of God; and painted it with Love. Now, God, to me, is capable only and always of Love, and I have the free will to let that love in or not. I, not God, inflicted the harsh penance I thought I deserved: my child for my sin. Catholicism really was a catalyst for my search for meaning in my life. That bedrock of suffering caused me to yearn for a better way: a way which ultimately led me to what I was missing—to UGLY, to self-love.

Patrick was the way and the light of my search. His wings fanned hope in me, encircled me with enough love, enough encouragement, enough backbone, to keep me moving forward when the going got so tough I thought I couldn't take another step. Without his support I might have become stranded somewhere along the way, and never initiated the search. Patrick and I parted, however, after fifteen years.

Chapter Sixteen

Sweet Healing

FOCUSED ON FINDING my daughter, I gave no thought beyond that. Totally unprepared for it, there I was, in the swirl of an adoptive family—an intrusive stranger, emotionally fidgeting, trying to find an inconspicuous niche to slip into when, in reality, there was no place to stand and no clear part to play.

Donna, the adoptive mother, already owned the leading role. Was I a stand-in for Donna, waiting in the wings in case she forgot her lines? It was confusing. *Danielle is mine; she's not, yet she is. What am I supposed to do? How am I supposed to act? What do I say?* Mostly I hid. I brought my unease and awkwardness with me. I sat in my head, a spectator, preoccupied with protecting myself, making a tape, running it over and over, telling myself *she is my baby, she is my daughter,* hypnotizing myself into believing it, for it felt foreign. *I'm her mother. I am not the mother. Who am I?* Incredulously, from a mixed-up brain, sanity on hold, I watched my daughter with her family—with faces that didn't fit.

Who is she? She was indubitably mine, knit to my very essence with intangible ties that begin and end in celestial domains unbreakable by time or distance. She was indubitably theirs, woven to them with time and the memories that fill scrapbooks. She was my stock, their mould; my genetics, their kin; my child, their family album. Mine, but also theirs, clearly apparent in childhood pictures that sucker-punched my heart when I first saw her so young shepherded by unfamiliar persons. The reality of handing over a helpless newborn, *my* helpless newborn, into the arms of strangers, hit me hard. The pain was worse than I imagined it would be.

Initially, I told Danielle I wanted to know from Donna everything about the baby and child she was. Then I changed my mind. It was too painful to tolerate someone else's memories of my baby. Annoyingly, with her adopted family, I slipped into the persona of the impotent, second-rate, unwed, pregnant sinner, interacting from that decrepit core, trying to hide, yet exposed. Even now, I occasionally forget that the nightmare I lived is in the past, because it has a way of plopping messily into the here and now, superimposing itself on the present with such stealth that the old familiar pain feels presently real. It can be hypnotic. With awareness that the past is back, I can choose to either entertain it, or stay present. Power is in the aliveness of the present moment—not the rotting body of the past.

I felt like a failure for giving Danielle up for adoption. Completely unaware of it, I had been trying to remedy that failure, be a mother, her mother, *the* mother: a second chance, a do over of sorts. But I wasn't remedying anything, I was making it worse. Because I didn't know how to take on that job, I was stirring up unnecessary emotional turmoil and allowing unwarranted responsibility to breed resentment that gobbled up love. *I'm supposed to be her mother but I'm not. I don't know how to be her mother. She already has a mother—but still it's my job. I can't be mother-ish, mother-like: that's not who I am. When I'm with her—that role just doesn't feel right. I'm dwarfed in a suit that's way too large for me, lost in it, tripping up in pant legs that are too long.* Seeing what I was covertly up to was such a breakthrough, and a great relief to release. Now there's room in its place for something to bloom and grow. Now, I'm grateful to simply be in her life.

I learned there is such a thing as failure of performance, distinct from personal failure. I failed to perform as a mother when I relinquished Danielle for adoption because I failed to take any action to circumvent it. Mistakenly, I believed I was a failure as a person because of it, and abdicated my power to an insatiable lie. There is tremendous freedom in letting go of the lie.

I am grateful for mustering the courage to take the road to find her. Danielle is far too precious to not have been found. She has definitely brought her special magic into my life. Invisible threads unite us and my heart is hinged to hers. We dance, sometimes fast, sometimes slow, sometimes I step right and she turns left, sometimes we crunch each other's toes; sometimes we sit one out. Still, we dance.

My search had nothing to do with Donna—it was never an attempt to replace her. I just wanted to find my daughter. My gift of Danielle to the hearts and lives of Donna and Rusty was the best gift they could have ever received. Donna had what my baby needed to live and thrive; she was ready and waiting for a stranger's child, sight unseen. I am grateful that a loving couple stepped up to dedicate their lives to Danielle when I could not. The way I see it, I gave Donna a cherished gift and she gave me the gift of cherishing it. No one needs a title in order to love. Donna and I are simply two women loving the same child. If I could have picked a mother for my child, I would have picked Donna.

You could say Donna and Rusty adopted Jacqueline and me, too. As honorary, extended family members, we are included in their family gatherings and celebrations.

When Brianne, Danielle's first child was born, my healing angel finally arrived. Brianne did not disappear after her birth although I was afraid she would. I knew babies could. Holding a newborn that came from my baby, a second chance to hold my own flesh and blood, heaven's lips bent down and kissed us both. Most weekends I kept that tiny creature overnight all to myself. I kissed, held, caressed and loved my baby's baby.

She is not Danielle. She will never replace Danielle. She is the closest I will ever come to living out what I missed. How did I get so lucky to have beautiful Brianne, the experience of loving her as I loved my baby, and heal the loss—at last? My inner child no longer stood crying at the gravesite of her child. She is complete. Brianne was the salve; she made it possible to heal the wound.

Next, along came her beautiful sister, Abigail, an active, curious bundle of absolute adventure. When Abigail falls down she rarely cries, hesitates momentarily, gets up and dives back into life. So young, she already knows that when you fall down in life you take a breath, get right back up, and get on with it.

It took me a long time to get back up and get on with it. It took me a long time to finally write on the outside everything that was written over and over on the inside. I had to embrace the repressed emotions and memories; talk about them; then write about them to be free. I wanted Danielle to know everything about my journey so that she too could be free. I have them both now; I have Jacqueline and I finally have Danielle. Brianne and Abigail are amazing additional blessings.

AUTHOR'S NOTES

BEFORE I KNEW that searching for my child was an option, my mind fondled the fanciful notion of writing a book. Danielle gave my fantasy cause. She gave me wings to fly, a reason to write it all down. What began as a quest to expose my life to my daughter—because in her shoes, I would want to know why my mother gave me away—became an incredible healing journey.

I gave Danielle away, an action so foreign to me now, I would deny myself capable of it; but I wanted her to know who I am. I wanted Danielle to know how my mind worked. Yet, my words and explanations seemed to miss her heart core when we spoke, and flew as question marks into the ethers, always leaving me wondering *if* she heard, *wha*t she heard, and what to say the next time we spoke. I put everything in writing because I wanted Danielle to know what conditioned my emotions at the time of her conception and birth. She told me she understood, but how could she with an unhinged vignette of a misshapen life?

My intention for this book broadened as I wrote, however, to include all who suffer from loss: that they may be instead over-taken by love; revel in the deliciousness of healing; and the sweet comfort of completion, for themselves, for those they love, and for their own lives.